Contents

CHAPTER 1

What you need to know about tax

This book is designed to help you make your tax situation as simple as possible and to allow you to feel in control of your finances.

For the purpose of this book, a pensioner is regarded as either a woman who is 60 or over or a man aged 65 or over, because it is at these ages that the tax and social security system in the UK triggers special allowances and different rules for calculating your tax status. That does not mean that people under those ages are ignored in this book – they are indeed catered for from time to time. For example, 60 is a significant age for both females and males as regards the Winter Fuel Payment, and also there are cases of people retiring before those ages because of ill health; again, this is a reason for special tax concessions and rules.

It should be stated here that the State Pension age for women is to be increased to 65 and is being phased in over a ten-year period between 6 May 2010 and 6 March 2020, so it will start to affect everyone born after 6 April 1950 (see Appendix 4).

The purpose of this book

In my view, the tax system in the UK deals harshly with people over retirement age. Although it gives pensioners higher tax allowances, it makes the calculations of any tax liability more and more difficult to cope with and this at a time, particularly for the elderly, when mentally, and perhaps physically, they don't want to be bothered with forms and red tape; and, more important, is the worry that can go with financial matters and often the feeling that you are being hounded by the Inland Revenue or given the sense that you have done something wrong. After all, if you have worked hard all your life you should be entitled to enjoy the fruits of your labours and not have to spend time battling with the tax office or spend time worrying about financial matters.

In addition to the special tax allowances and rules that apply to pensioners, in the last year or so there has been the introduction of Pension Credit, which in terms of calculation and paperwork is an administrative nightmare.

It seems that whereas the Government want to help pensioners, they go about it in such a convoluted way, always creating a forest of forms and red tape, that it is no wonder that millions of pensioners do not claim monies to which they are legally (and morally) entitled. Tens of thousands of pensioners don't claim because of the hassle, or because pride prevents them from claiming from the State to supplement their own income, even though they have probably paid tax and National Insurance contributions throughout their working life to enable them to claim benefits when they need assistance.

How to use this book

Throughout this book the main aim has been to be as practical as possible, avoiding superfluous words but still trying to keep things simple. After all, the legislation is complicated enough without this book adding to your burden.

Don't necessarily try reading this book from start to finish; certainly read the first two chapters because this is the key to understanding the basic rules for pensioners and their tax; but thereafter dip into each chapter when you want explanations or help with a particular problem.

Throughout the book there are many references to official helplines; don't be afraid to use these, for they are designed to offer practical help. But, if you do telephone them, do make sure that you have as many facts and figures as possible in front of you before you pick up the telephone – this will make the call easier for the helper to provide constructive assistance. Always make sure you have your National Insurance number (this is the key to most Inland Revenue and social security files and records), and if possible your tax reference number.

Tax rates and benefits change from year to year – and sometimes during the year; you can telephone the publisher's office at any time to get the latest tax rates, although obviously they can't answer your specific queries or problems. Telephone Foulsham on 01753 526769 and ask for the tax update office.

However, if you have any criticism of this book, or ideas as to how it could be improved, do please drop the author a line at the publisher's address, which is on the copyright page.

The basic elements of tax and pensions

The tax system in the UK is run by *H M Revenue & Customs*, the new department responsible for the business of the former *Inland Revenue*, which has now merged with the Customs and Excise. But because it has become Government policy over the last few years to integrate social security benefits with the tax system, the *Department for Work and Pensions,* incorporating The *Pension Service,* also have a finger in the communal pie! In this book, however, reference is made to the Inland Revenue under its old title as they are still in the process of updating their forms and leaflets, etc. to reflect the new agency name.

The tax year runs from 6 April in one year to 5 April in the next year. Annual tax returns are normally sent out to taxpayers in April each year. They are usually automatically sent out to all taxpayers who pay tax at higher rates; those who have complicated tax affairs or income from several sources; the self-employed; and those on whom the tax office just want to keep tabs!

However, the onus is on you to fill in a tax return if you owe tax or, better still, are due a refund; and the fact that you have not been sent a tax return is no excuse for not sending one in. Telephone your nearest tax office (see the *Yellow Pages* under Inland Revenue) and ask for them to send you a tax return – quote your National Insurance or taxpayer reference number.

Many people will tell you that the tax return is difficult to complete. Yes, it can be, but the secret is in making sure that you have all the information to hand before you start to fill it in; although there are many sections and questions in the form, people only have to answer a few, so don't approach this task with trepidation. If you want a simple guide to help you fill in your tax return, you will find my earlier books, *How to Fill in Your 2005 Tax Return the Easy Way* and/or *Check Your Tax and Money Facts* very helpful.

One of the reasons pensioners find tax aggravating is because there is a general misconception about the State Pension (including any additional and graduated pension), which is paid without tax deducted. Is it free of tax? Yes, it is if that is your only source of income, but your State Pension is added to any other income you have before arriving at your total income; you then deduct any tax allowances due to you and that then gives you your net total income on which you will pay tax at varying rates.

If you have a second or third pension from a past employer, you will find that tax is deducted from that before you receive it. The Inland Revenue will have issued your former employer (or the insurance company paying the pension) with a code number which will reflect your tax status and it will tell them how much tax to deduct. Quite often neither you nor the tax office will know at the beginning of the year what your total income is going to be from all sources for the next 12 months. They can only make a guess, and that is why it is important that you do check your total income and how much tax has been deducted at the end of the year to see if you can get a refund (which is often the case with pensioners) or whether you need to pay additional tax (see Chapter 4).

Summary – a helping hand

Over the past couple of years or so the tax system has become more confused as it evolves to reflect political agendas. In particular the introduction of Pension Credit and other credits, the major changes in the pension legislation which come into force in April 2006 (but which need to be considered before that date) and the confusion over equity release schemes have all added to the minefield for pensioners. This book will help you pick your way through the tax pitfalls and benefits.

CHAPTER 2

Are you *really* a taxpayer?

This chapter only deals with income tax. National Insurance (which is a form of taxation), capital gains tax and inheritance tax are dealt with in other sections of this book.

The fact that you may have had tax deducted from your pension payments or other income does not necessarily mean that you should be paying tax. You are only classed as a taxpayer when your *total net income* is more than your *tax allowances*. So, the key to understanding the tax system and arranging your affairs to make the most of things is to work out your total income.

Your total income level is also the deciding factor as to whether you can receive building society or bank interest without tax having been deducted (see page 68) and whether you can claim social security benefits, Pension Credits, council tax rebates and many other things.

So, make sure you know how your total income is calculated, because it's not as easy as it might first appear.

What is your total income?

Most of the types of income that you may receive are listed in Appendix 1 but not all have to be included in the total – those which you can ignore for this purpose have also been identified in that appendix.

You need to add up all your income to find your total income before reliefs for tax purposes. Undeniably, this is a very long list in the appendix! But there are obviously many sources from which an individual can get income and, as the object of this exercise is to establish your *total income for tax purposes* (and for other purposes as will be seen later), then it's important to get it right.

You would be understandably annoyed if you thought, for example, that your total income was below the limit for tax purposes and had not realised that you had to include, say, a Bereavement Allowance or Carer's Allowance.

So, now that you have established your overall income the next step is to deduct any *payments* that are allowed as a deduction for tax purposes.

Payments and reliefs you can deduct from your total income

You are allowed to deduct from your total income certain payments and reliefs before you calculate your tax.

These would include such things as:

- payments that you personally make into a pension scheme (if you are still paying into one).
- maintenance and alimony payments that you make if they are legally enforceable and you, or your former husband or wife, were born before 6 April 1935; the maximum is usually increased in each year's Budget (see Appendix 3), but such relief ceases if your former husband or wife remarries.
- allowable interest payments on qualifying loans – these are mainly for loans to buy shares or lend to closely controlled trading companies, partnerships, etc. or on loans to pay inheritance tax.
- interest on loans to buy an annuity if the person buying the annuity was aged 65 or over, the loan was secured on the individual's main residence in the UK or Republic of Ireland and the loan was taken out before 9 March 1999 (or other loans have replaced the original loan); relief is restricted to 22 per cent up to a maximum loan of £30,000.
- gifts to charity (see Chapter 12 for full details).
- contributions to Venture Capital Trusts and Enterprise Investment Schemes.

Your net total income

It is important to stress that the term 'total income' for tax and other purposes is your overall income less any tax reliefs and allowable payments. Note that reliefs are not the same as allowances.

A typical example of a calculation of total income after reliefs (referred to by the Inland Revenue as net statutory income for the purpose of calculating your age-related personal allowance) might be as follows:

	£
State Pension, say	3,926
Pension from former employer	5,640
Rent from unfurnished room after allowable expenses (not under Rent-a-Room scheme)	2,000
Casual work	780
	£12,346
Less: donation to charity under Gift Aid	350 (gross)
Total income after reliefs	£11,996

(Note that the Gift Aid deduction will not apply to a basic-rate taxpayer when actually calculating tax payable, as relief has already been given – see Chapter 12 for higher-rate taxpayers.)

Tax allowances and what they are *really* worth

There are three basic tax allowances: a personal allowance, which everyone receives automatically; a married couple's allowance (depending on your date of birth); and a blind person's allowance if applicable. The last two allowances you claim by filling in a tax return.

The amount of each allowance is announced in each year's Budget, normally in March so that it takes effect from the start of the following tax year on 6 April (see Appendix 3).

Personal allowance

From the moment that someone is born they are entitled to a basic personal tax allowance – the figure is £4,895 for 2005–2006. However, once you reach the age of 65, for the next tax year starting the following 6 April you are entitled to an age-related personal allowance of £7,090; and once you reach 75 then, again from the following 6 April, this age-related allowance goes up to £7,220.

These age-related allowances are, almost unbelievably, restricted depending on your net income level. The threshold for 2005–2006 is £19,500 and, for every £2 of income over that level, your allowance is reduced by £1; but no taxpayer can get less than the basic personal allowance of £4,895.

You cannot transfer this allowance to a husband or wife; if your income is insufficient to use it all, you lose it.

Married couple's allowance

This can be claimed for those born before 6 April 1935. The figures for 2005–2006 are £5,905 for those aged 65–74 and £5,975 for those aged 75 or over.

A wife can claim one-half of this allowance, or indeed the whole sum if her husband agrees, by filling in Inland Revenue form 18, available from any tax office. This must be submitted before the start of the tax year to which it is to refer. Relief can only be claimed at 10 per cent, however, and again the allowance is restricted: for every £2 of income over £19,500 for 2005–2006 the allowance is reduced by £1, with the minimum any taxpayer can get being £2,280 after taking account of any reduction in the personal allowance above. Note that if a person born before 6 April 1935 gets married after 5 April 2000 the allowance can still be claimed.

If you realise after the end of the tax year that you have not used all your married couple's allowance because your income is too low, it's not too late. The tax return includes a box you can tick to claim for any surplus allowances to be transferred to your husband or wife.

If you are widowed, you can claim any unused part of the married couple's allowance in the year of bereavement.

Blind person's allowance

A registered blind person can claim relief at 10 per cent on £1,610 for 2005–2006. This is also claimable by blind persons in the year preceding the year in which they were officially registered as blind if, at the end of the previous tax year, evidence was available to support the eventual registration.

The allowance is transferable to a husband or wife even if he or she is not blind if it is to your benefit and will reduce your tax bill, and the same procedure applies as for the married couple's allowance with regard to claims for transfer of surplus allowances.

Income tax rates

These are normally announced in the Spring Budget each year. For 2005–2006 there are four rates: a starting rate of 10 per cent, a basic rate of 22 per cent, a higher rate of 40 per cent and a savings rate of 20 per cent. The income level at which these rates come into effect is shown in Appendix 3.

Remember that the income band is after deducting any reliefs or allowable expenses and after deducting any tax allowances.

Summary of progress so far

You will have at last arrived at a total net income figure after deducting your tax allowances as above – and don't forget that a husband and wife each have their own tax allowances and each have to do their own tax calculations and complete separate tax returns.

To summarise

Total income, less reliefs and allowable payments less tax allowances, equals your net income for tax purposes.

If this is less than the starting-rate tax band (£2,090 for 2005–2006), you are not a taxpayer.

CHAPTER 3

Your tax return – and tax refunds

Why do so many pensioners pay too much tax?

One of the main reasons that pensioners pay too much tax is a rather innocuous piece of paper called form P161.

The Department for Work and Pensions tell the Inland Revenue when someone is due to reach the age of 60 or 65, and the tax office should send form P161 to the taxpayer to be completed and returned, but in fact only a small percentage of the forms are ever returned.

This is probably because the importance of the form is not made clear. The tax office need this form because it tells them what your likely income is going to be once you have retired (and where it is coming from). They can then apply a tax code number to recoup tax from any non-State-Pension income or earnings if you are carrying on working.

If they are not given this information, they may assume an incorrect level of State Pension, you may not get the age-related higher personal allowance and, indeed, you may not get the married couple's allowance if you are entitled to it.

The result is that you will pay more tax than you should and unless you check your tax situation each year (see Chapter 4) you will always be out of pocket.

What are PAYE codes?

If you are in paid employment, or have a pension other than the State Pension, then you will be allocated a code number which will tell your employer, or your pension provider, how much tax to deduct from your income or pension.

The tax office apply this based on the information you will have given them via either a tax return or your advising them as to your anticipated income levels for the current tax year.

This code number will be contained in a PAYE Coding Notice that will be sent to you, and the onus is on you to check it; your employer or pension provider will only be sent the actual code number, not the detail as to how it is calculated, so they cannot check it on your behalf.

The actual number represents your total tax-free pay, usually the total of your allowances, but in fact the last digit is omitted. For example, a code 683P means that you start paying tax after your income (from that particular source) reaches £6,830 (£131.35 a week).

The letter after your code number defines your status. For example, P means you are entitled to the age-related personal allowance if aged between 65 and 74, with V being used if you are also entitled to the married couple's allowance and you are on basic-rate tax; Y is used where you are entitled to the personal allowance and are aged 75 or over. With your Coding Notice there will be an explanatory leaflet.

Remember that if you receive the married couple's allowance (see page 11) the tax relief is only 10 per cent, so there will be a clawback figure in your Coding Notice to adjust this.

Too much tax deducted from your pension?

If you find that you are due a tax refund after checking your own tax, as explained in the next chapter, when you apply for a refund do remind the tax office to amend your PAYE code number.

One of the reasons that millions of pensioners have too much tax deducted from their State Pension or pensions they receive from their former employer, or from private pensions, is that the Inland Revenue don't always know at the beginning of a tax year what their total income from all sources is going to be for the forthcoming year.

They therefore give you a relatively low code number to make sure they get their pound of flesh in tax, on the basis that you can always reclaim tax if you have overpaid (they would rather you claim tax back than having to chase you for underpaid tax!).

Note that your PAYE coding will go to the supplier of your main pension if you have more than one, and tax at the basic rate will be deducted from any other private pension.

Should you complete a tax return?

The mere fact that the Inland Revenue have not sent you a tax return is no excuse for not completing one. The onus is on you, not the tax office. So, who should fill in a tax return?

You should usually complete a return if you are a higher-rate taxpayer, or you are in partnership or self-employed, or you have income or capital gains to declare on which tax is due. Otherwise, if you have paid the correct amount of tax or you are below the tax threshold, you do not have to send in a tax return. There is one caveat to that: if the tax office do send you a tax return, even if you do not owe any tax, you *have* to complete it and send it in. The Inland Revenue do this from time to time either just to update their records on your personal circumstances or because they may have reason to think that you are not declaring your income properly. They may also send you a form P810 to fill in every so often so they can keep track of changes in your income. The form requests basic information regarding your income and may be issued every three years.

Obviously, you also need to send in a return if you have paid too much tax because: you have had too much tax deducted from your pension; tax deducted from your other income means that you have overpaid after taking into account your tax allowances; or you have received casual income.

How do you get a tax return?

Telephone the tax office that deals with either your employer's or your pension provider's PAYE or, if you are self-employed or unemployed, contact your local tax office (see the local telephone directory under Inland Revenue).

Remember when asking for a tax return that there are several individual forms – a main return and then supplementary returns if you are employed, self-employed, own land or buildings, etc. Telephone 0845 9000 404 if you have the main tax return but also need supplementary sheets.

How to submit a tax return

You can complete a tax return either manually or online via a computer. There is a free telephone helpline manned by the Inland Revenue (0845 9000 444).

When telephoning, or indeed when making any contact with the tax office, always quote your tax reference numbers or your National Insurance number.

Manual tax returns

When you have filled in your tax return, do make sure that you have signed it – a surprisingly large number of taxpayers forget to do this (probably overcome by the sense of relief at having completed filling in the forms!) – and post it to the tax office shown on page one of the form. Keep a copy for reference.

If you send in your tax return by 30 September, the tax office will calculate any tax demand or refund for you and, if you are due to pay tax of less than £2,000 you can elect to pay it by instalments by having your PAYE code changed; otherwise the deadline is 31 January and you will be expected to do any calculations yourself (although you don't have to) but, as you will have to pay any tax demand in a lump sum by 31 January, you will not necessarily know how much to pay if you don't do the calculations yourself.

Online

You can either use the Inland Revenue free software package which you can download from www.hmrc.gov.uk (which will cover most tax forms but not all of them) or you can buy commercial software packages which have been approved by the Inland Revenue.

To register electronically with the tax office, log on to: www.online.inlandrevenue.gov.uk/ – you need your tax reference number or National Insurance number; there will then be a wait for about a week before you receive your ID and pin number. Once you have that, you can start filing.

The main advantages of filing electronically are that you have until 30 December (instead of 30 September) if you want any tax underpayment collected via your PAYE code number; the tax calculations are done automatically; any repayment is likely to be faster; and overall the service is safe, secure, available 24 hours a day and you can view your statement at any time.

Short tax returns

The Inland Revenue have tried to simplify the main self-assessment return by issuing what is called a short tax return. It is being sent to taxpayers whose tax affairs are fairly straightforward, but you cannot file it electronically. You don't have to use this form; if you would prefer a full tax return, or if you think the short return is inappropriate for your circumstances, telephone 0845 9000 444.

What if you have made a mistake?

If you realise that you have made a mistake in filling in your tax return, because you have forgotten to declare some income or claim an allowance, you can go back six years to rectify the situation by writing to your tax office. Obviously, if it transpires that you owe some more tax then you will have to pay it, plus interest, but on the other side of the coin if you have overpaid tax and are due a refund then you can claim this with interest.

Payments on account

If you have several sources of untaxed income, or you are self-employed, you will have to make two payments for the current tax year: one half on 31 January and the other half on 31 July, with any balance due, once your liability is calculated, on the following 31 January.

It is up to you to decide how much of your tax liability to pay on account. The tax office will suggest a figure and if you don't agree you can challenge it (by asking for and completing form SA303) but if you do and it subsequently transpires that you did not pay enough you will be charged interest. You will be sent a statement of account (form SA100) from time to time, which is also available for reference on the web site if you have registered to submit your tax return electronically.

Surcharges and penalties

If you do not send in your tax return by 31 January, you will be charged a penalty of £100 and a further £100 six months later if you have still not sent it in. You will also have to pay interest on late paid tax and an additional tax penalty of 5%, which the tax office refers to as a surcharge on any tax due for the previous year which was not paid by 28 February. An additional 5% is charged if the previous year's tax is still not paid by 31 July.

Keep your records safe

The law states that you must keep all your records of income, benefits, expenses, etc. – in fact everything supporting your tax return – for 22 months from the end of the tax year; this increases to five years and ten months from the end of the tax year if you are self-employed.

How to claim a tax refund

At the end of each tax year on 5 April, you should check to see exactly what income you received during the year and what tax you have actually paid – as shown in the next chapter.

To reclaim any tax overpaid, ask your tax office for leaflet IR110 and form R40. The leaflet gives some simple notes and you will need to complete the form, which is similar to a tax return but not as long, and return it to your tax office. There is no need to enclose dividend vouchers or interest statements, but the tax office may ask for them at a later date, so do keep them safe.

If most of your income has already had tax deducted from it (for example interest), you may be able to make quarterly, half-yearly or annual repayments; your tax office will advise you on this.

Even if you are a taxpayer, you may have had tax deducted at 20 per cent from interest received, and because you have not had the benefit of the 10 per cent tax band (see Appendix 3) you should claim a refund of the difference. There are a great number of pensioners on low incomes who are not making these claims.

Do remember that unless you send in a tax return you will not get any refund due to you. It does not come automatically because the tax office does not know if you have overpaid tax unless you tell them about your income and any tax that you have had deducted, by filling in a tax return.

CHAPTER 4

How to check your tax

You should check your tax situation at the end of each tax year – after 5 April. Even if your income is fairly low, it is surprising how many pensioners, in particular, pay more tax than they should; checking your total income and any tax deducted not only gives you the opportunity of claiming some tax back but also will give you a guide as to whether you might be eligible for Pension Credit, or social security benefits as explained elsewhere in this book.

Checking your tax

Appendix 3 gives a summary of tax rates and income levels. When you are checking your tax, make sure you use the correct set of figures for the year in question.

Here are some basic examples to show how you can work out your tax liability or indeed work out a tax refund if one is due to you. Note that in all cases the figures for 2004–2005 are used.

In the first example, Fiona has a fairly simple tax structure and only pays tax at the starting rate. In the second example, John has a higher income which takes him into the basic-rate tax bracket. In the third case, Michael's income is at a level where his age allowance is restricted. In the fourth case an example is shown for a married couple, Jack and Betty, which shows how the married couple's allowance is calculated.

In all these cases you can see how relatively simple it is to check your tax return rather than just relying on the Inland Revenue to get it right. The percentage of wrong tax assessments is surprisingly high so it is well worth putting aside a little time to check things yourself.

Example 1

Fiona (showing tax at the starting rate and how a tax overpayment has arisen)

Fiona is aged 71 and has a total State Pension of £4,300, and a pension from her former employer of £2,875 a year (from which tax of £550 has been deducted under PAYE).

Assuming the figures are for the year ended 5 April 2005, her tax liability is worked out as follows:

	£
State Pension	4,300
Other pension	2,875
	7,175
Less: age-related personal allowance	6,830
Net income for tax purposes	£ 345
Tax payable £345 at 10%	£34.50

But Fiona has already paid tax of £550 on her other pension, so she can claim back £550 less £34.50 = £515.50.

If Fiona has not had a statement from the Inland Revenue confirming that she is due a tax refund then she should ask the tax office for leaflet IR110 as explained on page 17 – or she could fill in a tax return requesting a refund at the same time.

Example 2
John (showing tax at basic rate and how a tax refund is calculated)

John is aged 76 and has a State Pension of £5,100, and a pension from a former employer of £4,540 (from which tax of £400 has been deducted under PAYE), and he gives £300 to his local church under Gift Aid. Assuming the figures are for the year ended 5 April 2005, his tax liability is worked out as follows:

	£
State Pension	5,100
Other pension	4,540
	9,640
Less: age-related personal allowance	6,950
Net income	£2,690

Tax payable:	£
£2,020 at 10%	202.00
£670 at 22%	147.40
	£349.40

John has already paid tax of £400 under PAYE so he can claim a refund of £50.60 (£400.00 less £349.40); see page 17.

In the above example the Gift Aid contribution is not actually deducted in the calculation because £300 is regarded as the net amount after tax, so basic-rate tax has already been allowed and the charity can reclaim this.

If John had been a higher-rate taxpayer, he could have claimed back the difference between 22 per cent and 40 per cent.

The way tax relief works on gifts to charity is explained in Chapter 12. A surprising number of taxpayers do not claim gift aid relief on their tax return.

Example 3
Michael (showing how the age related personal allowance is restricted)

Michael is aged 73. In the year ended 5 April 2005 he has a State Pension of £4,800, other pension income of £8,500 (from which PAYE of £1,700 has been deducted), and he received wages from a part-time job of £6,400.

His tax liability is worked out as follows:

		£
State Pension		4,800
Other pension		8,500
Employment		6,400
	£	19,700
Less: age-related personal allowance	6,830	
but restricted because of his income		
£19,700 – £18,900 × 50%	400	6,430
Total net income		£13,270

Tax payable:

	£	
2,020 at 10%	202	
11,250 at 22%	2,475	
13,270	2,677	
Less: tax already paid by deduction from his pension	1,700	
Remaining tax payable	£977	

When Michael submits his tax return, he will receive a tax assessment for this sum which he must pay by 31 January 2006.

Michael's tax liability arose because his employer did not deduct PAYE from his earnings from his part-time job. The Inland Revenue should issue a PAYE code to rectify this for the next year once they process Michael's tax return. An explanation as to how PAYE codes work and how they are issued is given on page 13.

Example 4

Jack and Betty (showing how the married couple's allowance is calculated and how a personal allowance is lost)

Jack is aged 77. In the year ended 5 April 2005 he received a State Pension of £4,800, and £7,000 other pension income (from which PAYE of £300 was deducted). He was born before 6 April 1935 so he can claim the married couple's allowance.

His wife, Betty (aged 76), has no income other than her State Pension, so as that is less than her age-related personal allowance of £6,950, she paid no tax; however, she will also lose the balance of this allowance as she has insufficient income to cover it. It cannot be transferred to Jack.

Jack's tax liability is worked out as follows:

	£
State Pension	4,800
Other pension	7,000
	11,800
Less: age-related personal allowance	6,950
	£4,850

Tax payable:	£	£
2,020 at 10%	202.00	
2,830 at 22%	622.60	
4,850	824.60	
Less: Married couple's allowance £5,795 at 10%	579.50	
Tax payable	£245.10	

Jack has paid tax of £300 already under PAYE so he can claim a refund of £54.90 (£300.00 less £245.10).

How do interest and dividends affect your tax?

Not all investment income is taxable: there are a lot of savings opportunities that are tax free (see Chapter 9). You do not have to include any free-of-tax income in your total income calculations, nor do you have to declare it on your tax return.

In the earlier examples, Fiona, John, Michael and Jack all had income, from either pensions or employment but no investment income so their tax calculations were fairly straightforward.

If you receive interest from, say, a building society or bank account, or dividends from stocks or shares, the tax system becomes a little more complex because you have to differentiate between non-savings income and savings income.

The reason for this is that savings income is taxed at a different rate (see Appendix 3), and indeed the way interest is taxed is different again from that which applies to *dividends*. It is so frustrating that the UK tax structure is so unnecessarily complicated.

What follows is the easiest way to set out your calculations if you have income from savings. To calculate your tax liability you need to break your income down into different chunks and always use the following sequence in doing the calculations. Make a list of your total income under the following headings:

1 **Non-savings income and benefits** (from which you deduct your allowances, expenses and pension payments). For the year ended 5 April 2005 this was taxed at 10 per cent up to £2,020; then at 22 per cent until the limit of the 22 per cent band was reached, then at 40 per cent.

2 **Non-dividend savings income:** Taxed at 10 per cent if the £2,020 maximum has not been used up in the above calculation; then at 20 per cent until the limit of the cumulative 22 per cent band is reached; then at 40 per cent.

3 **Dividend income:** Taxed at 10 per cent until the limit of the cumulative 22 per cent band is reached; then at 32.5 per cent.

Dividends are paid after deducting a tax credit, and in checking your tax you need to add this tax credit to the net amount you actually received to arrive at a gross figure to go in your total income calculation. This tax credit cannot be reclaimed if you are a non-taxpayer, as shown in the following example.

Example 5

Joan, who is under 65, had a part-time job and earned £2,500 for the year ended 5 April 2005, from which tax had not been deducted at source. She also received net interest from a building society of £2,000 (tax deducted £500).

	£	£
Non-savings income		2,500.00
Interest received	2,000.00	
Tax deducted (20% of £2,500)	500.00	2,500.00
Total income		5,000.00
Deduct personal allowance		4,745.00
		255.00
Tax liability: £255 at 10%		25.50
Less: tax deducted at source		500.00
Tax refund due		£ 474.50

If Joan had received net *dividend* income of £2,000 instead of building society interest, she would not have been able to reclaim the tax credit that would have been deducted from her dividend.

Here is an example to demonstrate the calculation sequence and to show how one partner can end up paying too much tax because personal allowances are not used.

Example 6

Roy is 66 and is married to Ann (aged 68). Let's assume Roy's income is as shown below for the year ended 5 April 2005. Ann had no income other than her State Pension of £2,475.
Roy's tax liability works out as follows:

		£
Non-savings income		
State Pension and other pension		
(PAYE deducted, say £600)		12,000.00
	£	
Savings income		
Interest from bank deposit (received)	432.00	
Tax deducted at 20%	108.00	
		540.00
Carried forward		£12,540.00

Brought forward		£12,540.00
Dividend income		
Dividends received	450.00	
Tax credit	50.00	
		500.00
Total income		13,040.00
Less: age-related personal allowance		6,830.00
Total net income		£6,210.00

Roy's tax liability will be as follows:

Tax on his non-savings income
£12,000 less personal allowance
   of £6,830 = £5,170

£	
2,020 at 10%	202.00
3,150 at 22%	693.00
5,170	895.00

Tax on his savings income
As the 10% band has been fully used above,
   this will be taxed at 20%: £540 at 20%   108.00

Tax on his dividend income

£500 at 10%	50.00
	1,053.00
Less: Married Couple's Allowance 10% × £5,725	572.50
Total tax due	£ 480.50

Roy has already paid tax of £600 by deduction on his pension, on his interest (£108) and dividends (£50) totalling in all £758, so he can claim a refund of £758 less £480.50 = £277.50.

Note that Ann was entitled to an age-related personal allowance of £6,830 but could only offset her State Pension of £2,475 so the balance of her allowance, £4,355, is lost.

Roy could have saved tax and received a bigger tax repayment if he had transferred some of his investments to his wife; Ann could then have used her personal allowance against this income and would still not have been liable to pay tax.

The 'age trap'

In the preceeding example, Roy and Ann paid too much tax because his wife was unable to use her personal allowance. Had he had a higher income, then this situation could have been worse because his Married Couple's Allowance and age allowance might have been restricted. Thousands of older taxpayers are caught in this trap each year. What can they do about it?

There are three main courses of action:

- Transfer income-bearing assets between married partners so that the partner whose income is getting the tax allowances restricted has a reduced income and the partner who is losing part (or all) of the personal allowance cuts the loss; alternatively, arrange to hold the assets in joint names so that the income is apportioned between you – this will also be beneficial for capital gains tax and inheritance tax, as mentioned elsewhere in this book. How can you do this? One partner gifts the investment or savings account to his or her partner by writing a simple letter of intent and changing the name of the account by advising the bank, building society, National Savings office or whoever; in the case of shares, write to the registrar of the individual company, requesting a transfer form.
- Sell some of your investments or savings and transfer them into tax-free investments like National Savings Certificates or ISAs (see Chapter 9 for tax-free investment options).
- Check to see if you can benefit by transferring the married couple's allowance (or blind person's allowance) between you and your partner or vice versa (see Chapter 2).

A word of warning: If one partner has transferred all their savings to their partner and one of them has to go into a care home, those savings could affect the amount of financial help that you get from the Department for Work and Pensions, or local authority.

Also remember that you can delay taking your State Pension if you don't immediately need that income; this could reduce your taxable income and perhaps prevent allowance restrictions or prevent you paying tax at a higher rate (see Chapter 5, page 32).

On the next page is an all-embracing example to show how allowances can be lost and more tax paid than is necessary.

Example of how to check your tax for 2004–2005

Mark is aged 73 and his wife, Mary, is aged 69.

	Mark £	Mary £
Income for 2004–2005:		
State Pension, say	4,726.00	2,350.00
Other pension, gross amount (tax deducted, say £1,400)	8,886.00	
Rent from letting unfurnished room (after expenses)	4,046.00	
Total non-savings income	17,658.00	2,350.00
National Savings Bank interest:		
Ordinary account £40 (the first £70 is not taxable)	–	
Investment account (gross)	–	75.00
Bank deposit interest – received £ 144.00		
Tax deducted before receipt 36.00	180.00	
Dividend income – received 1,800.00		
– tax credit 200.00	2,000.00	
Total income	19,838.00	2,425.00
Less: personal allowance 6,830.00		6,830.00
but restricted because of		(4,405.00)
Mark's income limit (see note)		unused
£19,838 – £18,900 = £938		allowance
× 50% 469.00	6,361.00	
Taxable income	£13,477.00	

Now refer to the easy three-point sequence list on page 24 so that you use the correct percentages in calculating your tax.

Mark's tax liability will be:		£
On his non-savings income £17,658		
Less: his allowances £ 6,361 = £11,297		
	£2,020 at 10%	202.00
	£9,277 at 22%	2,040.94
On his savings income	£180 at 20%	36.00
On his dividend income	£2,000 at 10%	200.00
		2,478.94
Less: married couple's allowance	£5,725 at 10%	572.50
Total tax liability		1,906.44
But he has already paid by deduction the following amounts of tax:		
On his other pension	£1,400.00	
On his bank interest	36.00	
On his dividends	200.00	1,636.00
Tax still to pay		£ 270.44

Notes
1. Mark's total income was £19,838; as the income age limit is £18,900, his allowances are reduced by 50 per cent (£1 for every £2 over this limit). This could have been avoided if some of his income-producing assets had been transferred to Mary, his wife.
2. It will be seen that Mary had insufficient income to cover her personal allowance. The unused balance is lost – it cannot be used by her husband. It would have been more sensible for her to have received a greater part of the family income in order to reduce Mark's tax liability, so they should consider reorganising their investments to avoid the same problem happening next year.
3. Perhaps Mark should also have let the room furnished instead of unfurnished, with the lodger sharing the house so that the rent could have been received tax free under the Rent-a-Room scheme (see page 57).

If Mark and Mary were working out their likely tax situation for 2005–2006, they would still get the married couple's allowance (increased to £5,905). The age income limit would be £19,500 and the basic rate of tax stays the same at 22 per cent.

It will still be important for Mark to transfer some income-bearing investments to his wife, but she should not receive dividends as she cannot reclaim the tax credit if her income remains below her personal allowance; investments paying interest tax free would be preferable.

Tax assessments from the tax office

The way in which the above examples have been set out is the simplest way, and the method most professional accountants would use. Unfortunately, our tax system always makes things as complicated as possible and the statements you receive from the tax office will present the details in a different format. They tend to work backwards, allocating income against tax bands.

However, the net result should be the same and if it is not and you cannot see why there is a difference, write to your tax office and enclose a copy of your workings so they can identify the problems.

CHAPTER 5

The State Pension and what to do when you retire

The State Pension

You cannot claim the State Pension until you have reached the official retirement age of 65 for men and 60 for women. If you have retired earlier than these ages, you continue to be treated as a taxable individual and you cannot claim the tax concessions available to pensioners until the official retirement age.

If a married woman reaches 60 before her husband, she can only claim the full pension if she has paid sufficient National Insurance contributions in her own right, otherwise her pension will be reduced according to her contributions. There is legislation in place that will gradually increase a woman's retirement age to 65 – this affects all women born after 6 April 1950 – and details of the age graduation and pension rights are shown in Appendix 4.

In order to claim the full State Pension you have to have paid (or had credited) National Insurance contributions for a minimum number of years – the qualifying periods are 44 years for a man, and 39 years for a woman.

If you have received Jobseeker's Allowance or Incapacity Benefit, National Insurance contributions are credited to your account even though you have not been earning during these periods; similarly, people claiming Home Responsibilities Protection need fewer qualifying years to build up to get their pension, etc.

If the State Pension is your only source of income, you should apply to your local Department for Work and Pensions to supplement your income; you should also claim the Pension Credit (see Chapter 8), formerly called the Minimum Income Guarantee. The State Pension, together with any SERPS (State Earnings Related Pension Scheme) supplement and the Widow's Pension, do not have tax deducted from them before you receive them and, if your total income is higher than your allowance, you pay tax on the excess income.

SERPS has now been abolished but you do not lose your established entitlement either if you have retired or have not yet reached retirement age. It has been replaced by what is called a *State Second Pension (S2P)*; this is very much geared to boosting the pension rights of low earners and those with major disabilities.

Your State Pension may be enhanced by any Graduated Retirement Benefit which you may have earned from 1961 to 1975, plus any SERPS pension earned since that date if you were not contracted out.

Payment of the State Pension is by direct payment to a bank, building society or post office account, but there is a facility for people who are ill or disabled to receive their pension by cheque.

Telephone The Pension Service on 0845 300 1084 if you are four months from retirement and have not had a letter from them advising you of your pension entitlements. (See also page 13 – Why do so many pensioners pay too much tax?)

Home Responsibilities Protection

If you have been unable to keep regular work because you have had to stay at home to care for children or a disabled or elderly person and therefore have not made all the necessary National Insurance contributions in order to qualify for the full State Pension, you can benefit by claiming Home Responsibilities Protection. This is available to men and women, single or married. To claim, ask for form CF411 at your local social security office. They will also give you an explanatory booklet, because there are rules and regulations as to the age of the child, or period of disablement for an elderly person, etc.

If you have responsibility for looking after children under the age of 16 (or 18 if they are in full-time education), you should also claim the Child Tax Credit (see Appendix 2). Child Benefit should also be claimed. The Department for Work and Pensions publish a guide, *State Pensions for Carers and Parents* – telephone 0845 731 3233 to get a copy.

Women paying reduced rate

Married women had the option of paying a reduced-rate National Insurance contribution from 1948 to 1977, but none of these contributions counted towards a basic pension or, to be precise, they contributed very little (about 8p a week!). They only entitled you to certain health benefits.

Widows

A widow can benefit from the contributions that her husband had made under the National Insurance legislation provided she is under the age of 60 and has not remarried. Once a widow has reached 60, the State Pension would not be affected by remarriage. Widows can also claim 50 per cent of any State Second Pension (S2P) based on their late husband's earnings.

Divorced or separated

If you are a divorced woman and not entitled to a full State Pension, you may be able to claim under your former husband's contributions. Check with The Pension Service on 0845 60 60 265.

Postponing your State Pension

As from 6 April 2005 you can delay taking your State Pension for as long as you wish (prior to that date the maximum was five years) and get either an extra payment added to your pension for each year of postponement, or a lump sum.

Why would you want to postpone? Well, if you have enough income to live on at the moment then receiving the State Pension may put you into either a higher tax bracket or into the age trap scenario (see page 27) and it would be beneficial to delay taking that extra income until perhaps your other income is at a lower level.

Since 6 April 2005 there have been three options available as regards your State Pension entitlements once you reach official retirement age:

(a) You can retire and claim your State Pension.

(b) You can carry on working and claim your State Pension.

(c) You can delay claiming your State Pension – whether you are working or not.

If you decide to delay claiming, you have a further two options to consider:

(d) You can earn extra State Pension that will be added to your normal entitlement when you do decide to claim; the extra amount will be equivalent to 1 per cent of your weekly pension for every five weeks you put off claiming. Prior to 6 April 2005 you could only defer a pension for up to five years, but since that date there is no maximum period.

or

(e) You can claim a one-off lump sum payment based on the amount of State Pension you would have received in the period you have put off claiming, plus interest; this interest rate will be 2 per cent above the Bank of England's base rate.

You can only opt for the lump sum option if you put off claiming for at least 12 consecutive months.

The phrase 'State Pension' includes any earnings-related State Pension (SERPS) or S2P (State Second Pension) and any Graduated Retirement Benefit.

Tax position on lump sum payment

This lump sum payment needs to be added to your total income for tax purposes, and if this total exceeds your personal allowance you will pay tax on it.

However, the proposal before Parliament, which had not yet become law at the time this book went to press, is that the inclusion of any lump sum will only be taxed at the tax rate applicable to your other income; in other words, if you are in the 10 per cent band and the addition of a lump sum would take you into a 22 per cent band, the lump sum will only be taxed at 10 per cent.

The Pension Service will deduct tax from the lump sum payment – you will have to fill in a form stating what you think your total income will be for the year so they can decide what rate of tax to deduct. Sadly, this is yet another set of bureaucratic rules to cope with what should have been a fairly sensible and straightforward matter!

In the draft legislation it is also stated that any lump sum will not affect your entitlement to the age-related personal tax allowance. The lump sum will be excluded from your savings total when calculating any savings-credit part of the Pension Credit.

Even if you are already receiving the State Pension you can elect to stop receiving it and adopt one of the above options.

The Pension Service has published a booklet under the snappy title, *Your State Pension Choice – Pension now or extra pension later. A Guide to State Pension Deferral.* Telephone 08457 313 233 for a copy. There are also various web sites which give more information: www.over50.gov.uk, www.agepositive.gov.uk, and www.jobcentre plus.gov.uk.

Working after retirement

If you carry on working after the official retirement age, you can still claim the State Pension but you do not have to pay any more National Insurance contributions. Employers still have to contribute, however, which is somewhat unfair because no one benefits from their contributions except for the fact that the Government get even more revenue!

Stopped working prior to retirement age?

Check your State Pension quote – have you paid enough contributions? (See page 30). You can pay voluntary contributions to top up if necessary. You can't claim State Pension before retirement age but you can instead consider claiming Jobseeker's Allowance, Incapacity Benefit, Income Support, Housing Benefit and Council Tax Benefit.

Self-employed pensions

As with employed people, you have to notch up the required amount of National Insurance contributions in order to get the full State Pension, so do contact The Pension Service telephone helpline or web site to get a pension estimate to see how you stand (see below). You do not get the SERPS or State Second Pension if you are self-employed, so you will be particularly dependent on a personal pension scheme (see Chapter 6).

Pension forecast

At any time during your lifetime, until you retire, you can ask for a State Pension forecast. There are three ways to do this:
- Write to the Retirement Pension Forecasting Team, The Pension Service, Whitley Road, Newcastle upon Tyne NE98 1BA. They will send you a form BR19 to complete and then send you the forecast details.
- You can download the above form from their website at www.thepensionservice.gov.uk.
- You can call 0845 3000 168 and they will fill in the form for you over the telephone.

Whichever way you choose, make sure you get the forecast in writing so that you can refer to it; and you can keep doing this every few years if you want to see how things are progressing.

What to do when you retire

If you have been paying PAYE, you will receive a form P45 from your employer. Send this to the tax office (whose address will be shown on the form) with a letter confirming that you have retired, giving details of any pensions you will receive and telling them that you are not intending to take further employment. (See also page 13 which covers code numbers generally.)

If you decide to get employment again in the future, either full time or part time, you will have to ask your tax office for another code number.

If you have been self-employed, make sure your tax returns are up to date and tax liabilities agreed, and inform the tax office of your retirement.

The tax position on pensions

The State Pension, and supplementary pensions from either Graduated Contributions, SERPS or S2P, are all paid without tax being deducted, but they are all added to your total income in establishing whether you are a taxpayer (see Chapter 2).

New pension legislation

If you have contracted out of the Government State Second Pension (S2P), you will be able to take advantage of the new pension legislation that comes on stream in April 2006.

At present you cannot take benefits from an S2P (previously called SERPS) fund until the age of 60; but from 6 April 2006 you may be able to take this pension from age 50 and in addition take a 25 per cent tax-free lump sum, using the balance to purchase an annuity. This 'aged 50 plus' option lasts until 2020 at which time the minimum age will rise to 55.

Some of the legislation covering the options on these 'rebate only' or 'protected rights pensions', as they are called, is still to be clarified, so keep an eye on the financial pages of your newspaper in case they affect you.

CHAPTER 6

Pension schemes

By the time you have purchased this book you may have retired and already be in receipt of a pension, in which case you may need to skip this chapter and concentrate on other sections of the book.

However, if you have retired you may not have taken your pension but have left it in the pot to grow, or indeed you may be on the verge of retiring and need to consider what options are open to you.

This is why it is necessary to cover this area in some detail even in a book such as this, which is essentially to do with tax. The introduction of new pension legislation, which aims to simplify the tax and pension rules and regulations, has thrown the pension industry into short-term turmoil. The basic elements and options are covered in this chapter and the next.

Obviously it is not possible to go into great depth here on all schemes – there are other books on the market that just concentrate on these issues and will be more comprehensive. In this chapter I go to the top of the mountain, as it were, and summarise generally the options and decisions with which you have to contend.

The pension scene is currently unbelievably complicated. The variety of pension schemes and the rules and regulations governing them can vary considerably, and the tax ramifications are a minefield.

Type of pension scheme and the tax position (pre-April 2006)

There are several types of pension scheme although, once 6 April 2006 has passed, under new legislation (detailed in the next chapter) the difference between them will be substantially reduced. It is necessary, however, to cover them at this stage because in discussing the new pension rules later on, the definitions of existing schemes have to be identified.

Final salary scheme (also known as *defined benefit* or *salary-related schemes*) are an employer's scheme that guarantees a certain pension regardless of investment conditions based on a formula on what you have been earning, with a tax-free lump sum which may be up to or higher than 25 per cent of the fund value. The maximum pension you can have is two-thirds of your final salary.

Occupational money purchase schemes (also known as *defined contribution schemes*) which would include company pension schemes, executive pension schemes and small self-administered schemes (SSASs), provide for contributions being made to your employer's scheme which are accumulated with interest and used to buy your pension. The amount of the pension (an annuity) will depend on the amount paid in, how long-term investments have performed, current interest rates at the time of retirement, your age, and whether you are male or female. The maximum pension that can be taken is two-thirds of your final earnings at retirement.

The maximum total employee contribution levels allowed for tax is 15 per cent of your earnings (including taxable benefits); the extent of your employer's contribution will depend on the type of scheme, your age, length of service, etc.

Additional contributions

You can top up payments over and above any contribution being paid into your main employer's scheme (called Additional Voluntary Contributions – AVCs) getting tax relief by the contribution being deducted from your salary before PAYE is calculated; or you can pay into a separate scheme (called Free-Standing Additional Voluntary Contributions – FSAVC) and get tax relief by deducting tax at basic rate when you pay the premium – any higher rate relief being claimed by filling in boxes 14.10 or 14.11 in your tax return.

The 15 per cent annual limit referred to above has to include these additional contributions

Personal pension plans, which will include Self-Invested Personal Pensions (SIPPs), are pension schemes either taken out by you if you are self-employed or, if employed, you are not a member of an employer's scheme as defined above. Employers can also operate group personal pension schemes.

The maximum annual contributions are shown in the table on page 39. Tax relief is normally obtained by deducting tax at basic rate from the premiums, with any higher-rate tax relief being claimed by filling in Q11 in your tax return, the exception being the group personal pension schemes where the contribution will be deducted from your salary before tax is calculated. There is no limit to the total amount that can be accumulated in your pension scheme.

Stakeholder pensions are considered as personal pensions. These have been available since 6 April 2001 and are mainly intended to encourage middle- to low-earners to save for retirement. They were designed with flexibility in mind; the main provisions follow:

- All employers with five or more employees must offer these pensions if there is no existing pension scheme.
- The maximum gross annual contribution for non-earners is £3,600 but employees and the self-employed can pay more, based on their earnings.
- You can still take out a stakeholder pension even if you already have another personal pension or retirement annuity contract, provided the total contributions are within the limits (see table on page 39).
- There is freedom to switch to other pension providers without penalty, and charges are capped.
- You can make regular payments or just a single contribution and you can stop and start when you like.
- You can pay into a stakeholder pension at any age up to 75, even if you are not working, and you, or indeed anyone else on your behalf, can pay into a stakeholder pension, so you could pay into such a pension on behalf of your wife, husband, partner, children, grandchildren, etc. although the child cannot get money out of the scheme until he or she is 50 years old! (this will increase to 55 under the new legislation).
- The maximum management charge is 1 per cent a year.
- You can take a lump sum on or after retirement of 25 per cent, and the balance as an annuity.

You get tax relief by deducting tax at basic rate from the payment, and any entitlement to higher-rate tax relief you claim by filling in boxes 14.6 to 14.9 in your tax return.

If you are a member of an occupational pension scheme, or are a controlling director, you cannot contribute to a stakeholder pension if you earn over £30,000 a year.

Retirement annuity contracts also come under the category of personal pensions. These existed prior to 1 June 1988 and are also known as Section 226 pensions in Inland Revenue jargon. See the table on page 39 for contribution limits. You get tax relief by filling in boxes 14.1 to 14.5 in your tax return.

FURBS

A Funded Unapproved Retirement Benefit Scheme (FURBS) is a type of pension established under a trust and is more normally used to supplement conventional pension schemes for senior employees and directors. The main advantage is that they operate outside the Inland Revenue earnings limits and regulations associated with approved pension schemes, and normally there are no limits on tax-free withdrawals. However, contributions made by an employer are taxable on the employee and the fund is taxed on its income and growth.

A detailed analysis of FURBS is outside the scope of this book, but further information can be found on most financial web sites.

How much can you contribute to a personal pension scheme?

As mentioned above, there are limits set by the Inland Revenue depending on whether you are employed or self-employed, the level of your earnings and your age.

Maximum personal pension contribution limits

Age at beginning of tax year	Personal pension plan percentage of income	Retirement annuity premium percentage of income
up to 35	17.5	17.5
36 to 45	20.0	17.5
46 to 50	25.0	17.5
51 to 55	30.0	20.0
56 to 60	35.0	22.5
61 to 75	40.0	27.5

Earnings limits

For plans taken out after 14 March 1989 the maximum net relevant earnings figures on which relief is available are as follows: £95,400 for 2001–2002; £97,200 for 2002–2003; £99,000 for 2003–2004; £102,000 for 2004–2005 and £105,600 for 2005–2006.

Note: Earnings for both these calculations and for lump sum calculations include any taxable benefits (e.g. company car, fuel, health schemes) included in your P11D form.

With the new pension legislation operative from 6 April 2006, the limits become obsolete after that date.

Carry back pension payments to a previous tax year

In your tax return you have the opportunity to carry back to a previous year all or part of any amount you pay into a pension scheme if it is to your benefit tax-wise, provided that by so doing you don't exceed the maximum-allowed total contributions for that year.

In the case of personal pensions, including stakeholder pensions, you have until 31 January to make the payment and elect to backdate it. The decision must be made at or before the time of payment.

In the case of retirement annuity contracts you have an extra 12 months to decide whether you want to backdate to a previous tax year. So, for a premium paid in the 2005–2006 tax year, you will have until 31 January 2007 to elect for this to be carried back to 2004–2005.

There is a section in your tax return for you to make these options (see Q14). You also need to fill in forms PP43 and PP120, available from your tax office.

Note, however, that these carry-back opportunities will be scrapped from April 2006 when new rules to simplify pensions come into operation.

Pension scheme options on retirement

Prior to your retirement you will get a communication from your employer or your employer's pension advisers as to the amount of your pension, any Additional Voluntary Contributions (AVCs) you have made, the date pension payments will be made, any lump sum options and variations on the pension quote to cope with details of any Widow's or Widower's Pensions if you die first; and, indeed what payments will be received if you die fairly soon after you have retired. Inflation protection must also be considered.

On your retirement, you can usually take a tax-free cash lump sum payment, the calculation of which will depend on the type of scheme mentioned above. Members of defined benefit schemes don't have to worry about shopping around for the best pension (annuity) rates because the scheme trustees will purchase them for their members under a bulk deal. However, if you have exceptionally bad health, have a history of heavy smoking, are obese or have other health factors, then it is worth mentioning this fact to the trustees for they may be able to arrange a higher pension rate for you.

On the other hand, if you are not in a defined benefit scheme you will have to consider what annuity and/or income draw-down options are open to you.

Purchasing an annuity (pre-April 2006)

If you are in a personal pension scheme or an occupational money purchase scheme, when you come to retire, the money in your fund has to be used to purchase an annuity. You have to do this by age 75; or you can opt for income draw-down options (see page 42).

Annuities

An annuity is a guaranteed income for life. There are many types of annuity. You can, for example, purchase an annuity for a guaranteed period (say, five or ten years) in which case even if you die early the income will continue for a fixed period; or you can purchase an annuity whereby on your death an income continues for the lifetime of a remaining partner.

Annuity income is considered as part of your total income (see Chapter 2) and, depending on your overall income level, will be subject to tax. Normally the annuity provider will deduct tax before you receive the money – the amount of tax deducted will be governed by a tax code number which you need to check each year (see Chapter 4). Bear in mind that once you have elected to purchase an annuity then it has no ongoing transfer value.

Open market option

According to latest surveys, about 65 per cent of members of pension schemes assume that the annuity quoted by the company that runs the scheme is the best on offer and that they have to take what is offered without any questions asked.

This is not so. Under legislation, pension providers have to advise you that you do have the option of shopping around for the best annuity. Often this can result in an increase in annuity income by as much as 10 per cent. So be advised: shop around and get other quotes; you have no obligation to stay with your present pension provider.

If you are in any way medically impaired (a smoker, obese, etc.) you can get a quote for what is called an impaired life annuity, which can result in your getting a much higher annuity income – basically because the insurance company considers your life expectancy lower than average.

Frequency of income

In getting an annuity quote you can elect to have it paid monthly, quarterly, half-yearly or annually. There will be a difference. For example, it is estimated that an annuity paid annually in arrears compared to monthly in arrears will be around 4 per cent higher; but then, of course, you will be without money for a year, so it rather depends on what you plan to do with the annuity when you receive it.

Purchased annuities

Most people only resort to buying an annuity because, once you have taken your tax-free lump sum from your pension pot, the law requires that an annuity is purchased with the remainder of the fund. You can, however, buy an annuity in your own right (with your own capital as it were) and this is called a purchased annuity.

The tax structure is different from a pension scheme annuity in that part of the annuity is regarded as a return of capital and part is regarded as income. This income part is taxed by the Inland Revenue as part of your total income and will have had tax at the savings rate deducted from it before you receive it. Any tax so deducted can be offset against your other tax liabilities.

The apportionment as between capital and income will depend on your age and sex and will be shown in the quote you get from the insurance company.

Do seek professional advice

Your pension option is the most important decision of the retirement segment of your life, so don't resist getting professional advice if you have anything but a simple set of parameters. Regarding current annuity values, you can see most of them quoted in the national press or on the Internet at www.betterannuities.co.uk.

Income draw-down (pre-6 April 2006)

Under existing pension legislation you do not have to draw your pension from your fund(s) when you reach retirement age; you can let the investment in the pension fund grow (or not, depending on the performance of investment markets!) without your making further contributions. But you do have to commit to buying an annuity by the time you reach age 75 (see above).

An alternative to buying an annuity is to leave your pension pot invested, but to draw an annual income from the fund. This is known as income draw-down. It is considered that you need a pension fund of a minimum of £150,000 to make this a practical proposition.

The Inland Revenue lay down limits on the amount of income you can take from income draw-down schemes – the maximum amount is 100 per cent of the annuity amount you could purchase at retirement (pension companies will give you an actuarial quote), and the minimum is 35 per cent of that figure.

Income draw-down does not obviate your having to purchase an annuity at age 75; it merely delays it.

Bear in mind that by drawing an annual income under income draw-down you will gradually deplete the capital invested. With annuity values relatively low at present and with people living longer, there is an element of risk in these schemes. Most professional advisers would advise caution in considering these.

If you get an income under these schemes, it will be considered as part of your total income for tax purposes and, depending on your overall income level, you may have to pay tax on it.

Death benefits from your pension fund(s) (pre-April 2006)

It depends on the type of pension scheme as to what happens to the monies in your pension fund when you die. Under personal pension schemes the value of the fund is returned to your estate (free of income tax normally) to be distributed according to your instructions (usually contained in your will – see Chapter 13).

It is similar for money purchase and defined benefit schemes except that there is a maximum of four times salary, with the term 'salary' including taxable benefits that you may have been receiving (e.g. company car, fuel, private health insurance). Any excess over this maximum is paid as a pension to your partner or dependants, and will be added to their income and therefore be taxable if their total income is above the tax thresholds (see Appendix 3).

It will be appreciated that this is a general overview. It must be remembered that all pension schemes have their own trust deeds and variations of benefits, distributions, etc.

What happens to your pension if you are in the middle of a draw-down option and you should die? If you are married, your partner can cancel the draw-down facility and take the pension fund as a lump sum, but note that it will be taxed at 35 per cent.

What happens if your pension provider or employer goes out of business?

The last few years have been very volatile in the pensions industry, mainly due to the sharp fall in share prices, the mis-selling syndrome and more stringent regulations by the financial services authorities and the Government; or simply because your scheme has been inefficiently run.

Most pension companies have reduced their pay-outs and pension levels, so lots of people will receive, or are receiving, much less than they had expected and budgeted for. Even worse, some companies (and the fact that they were big has not provided the protection that many had expected) have actually gone into liquidation and been wound up; and it's not only pension companies, but also your ex-employer who was running your pension scheme, that may go under as well.

The Pension Protection Fund came into effect on 6 April 2005 but only covers the first £25,000 of expected annual pension income (or £27,778 a year for people who have retired at normal pension age) and only applies to schemes that go under after 6 April 2005. Those already trapped in failed schemes will have to rely on the less generous assistance from the Financial Assistance Scheme (FAS), which has a maximum payment of £12,000 and this is only paid to those within three years of retirement.

This will include a 50 per cent Widow's Pension provision; that's 50 per cent of the FAS benefit, not how much you would have been paid under your pension scheme prior to its going under. This is only applicable to surviving spouses of those who died if they were within three years of their scheme's retirement age on 14 May 2004 – although this is being revised by the Government.

Early retirement

It depends on your scheme's rules but either way the minimum age of 50 (increasing to 55 from 2010 under new legislation) will be the earliest you can retire, and your pension will be greatly reduced because of the greater span of years for which an annuity is likely to be paid. If you retire early in an occupational pension scheme, you have to leave the employment; in the case of a personal pension scheme or stakeholder scheme this is not the case and you can in fact continue working for that company after retirement.

If, however, you have to retire due to incapacity (either physical or mental), then the likelihood will be that you can claim the rate of pension that you would have got had you continued to normal retirement. But in the case of final salary schemes the maximum rate payable will be based on your salary level at early retirement date rather than what you would have been earning had you continued until normal retirement age.

The legislation covering early retirement due to ill health is not well defined, added to which the interpretation of your own pension scheme rules by the trustees may vary considerably from company to company. In this respect the Pensions Ombudsman is receiving a lot of disputes on which to adjudicate at the present time.

Divorced or separated person's rights

The law has changed materially over the last few years. Nowadays the pension pot (whether it be a company pension scheme, a stakeholder pension, a personal pension or an AVC scheme) accumulated by a husband or wife can be split between them as part of a divorce settlement.

This is not automatically done – it is all part of the divorce settlement and it seems rather to depend on the efficiency of the solicitor acting for each party as to whether this option is brushed aside when everyone is perhaps concentrating on things like the house, children's welfare, etc. against a background of emotional instability. So remember to raise the pension issue even if you are relatively young at the time of the divorce. It can be a very valuable asset in the mix of things in the longer term.

Old pension schemes – how to trace pension schemes from former employers

Most people have worked for several employers in their lifetime and the likelihood is that you will have been a member of a pension scheme run by one or more of those former employers. It is not uncommon, although in retrospect perhaps surprising, that many people don't keep records of contributions that they have made to former employers' pension schemes. But they could be valuable, so it is worth casting your mind back and contacting your former employer to ask for details; you will need to provide details of the dates that you worked for them and/or your National Insurance number. Alternatively, contact an organisation by the name of the Pension Schemes Registry, who can trace past pension schemes for you; they can be contacted by telephoning 0191 225 6316. Their web site is www.thepensionsregulator.gov.uk/.

It is most likely that there is value in past pensions, even though they may have been frozen when you left that employment.

Part-timers

Part-timers had few rights to equal consideration as regards their pension rights until a new legal ruling came into force in February 2001. If you can prove that you were treated unfairly concerning admission to a pension scheme or whatever, then you can apply to an Employment Tribunal either before you leave your employment or within six months of leaving.

The tax position has been somewhat vague on any backdated pension awarded. It appears that no tax relief can be claimed on the backdated pension contribution if employees have moved to another employer or have since retired. The fairness of this ruling is difficult to understand, but such is the law!

Pension Credit

The Pension Credit was introduced in October 2003. It replaced the Minimum Income Guarantee. Full details of this complicated piece of legislation, how to calculate your credit and how to claim are dealt with in Chapter 8.

CHAPTER 7

New pension legislation

The previous chapter covered the existing pension legislation prior to 5 April 2006 and also dealt with many general pension matters. The Pensions Act 2005 has now radically changed the pensions scene.

Originally the new pension legislation was going to take effect from 6 April 2005 but this was delayed and now the relevant date is 6 April 2006. *This date is now known in the pensions industry as 'A-Day'.*

The new legislation will make pensions easier to understand and will do away with the inexplicable differences that seemed to exist between company pension schemes and personal pension schemes – and lots of other schemes in-between!

There are currently eight different statutory pension rules and regulations, and the new Pensions Act will amalgamate all of these into one set of rules for all schemes.

Apart from a general simplification, the new legislation covers the age at which you can retire, the levels of contributions, the tax-free amounts you can receive from pension schemes, the other benefits payable and the investment opportunities.

You will be able to pay into more than one pension scheme from A-Day. Prior to that, this option was only available if your earnings were less than £30,000 a year and you were not a controlling director – then you could pay up to £3,600 into a personal or stakeholder pension scheme in addition to a company pension scheme.

The new legislation and a comparison with existing rules is considered below.

Retirement age

The minimum retirement age at which you can start to take pension benefits will be raised from 50 to 55 from 2010. From 6 April 2006, members of employer pension schemes will be able to take their pension and still continue to work in the same way as personal pension scheme members have been able to prior to the new legislation.

You will not, therefore, need to retire to receive benefits, subject to any overriding regulations in your pension scheme. This may enable members of money purchase and final salary schemes to retire earlier than 60 or 65, which is usually the stipulated age, and also give opportunities for phased retirement.

Tax-free cash

Under the new pension legislation you can take a maximum tax-free cash sum of 25 per cent of the fund value, the remainder of the fund being used to buy an annuity. This effectively means that those with personal pensions may be able to take 25 per cent of the fund as tax-free cash even if the amount under the old rules had shown a lower percentage entitlement.

In the case of money purchase and final salary schemes, if your tax-free cash is greater than 25 per cent you may need to register this to protect those rights; if tax-free cash is lower than this percentage, you may be able to defer your benefits until after A-Day when the tax-free cash maximum of 25 per cent may be taken.

Also, if you retire after A-Day, Additional Voluntary Contributions may be allowed to be taken into the tax-free cash equation – this was not so under the old legislation.

The value of your pension funds

Prior to 5 April 2006 there has been no limit on the amount that you can have in your personal pension pot, nor indeed in money purchase company pensions, although these have a restriction on the amount of pension income you can take (as detailed in Chapter 6).

From A-Day, however, your pension fund value (all of your pension funds if you have more than one) will be capped at £1.5 million, gradually rising to £1.8 million in 2010–2011. Any value above this will be subject to a Lifetime Allowance Charge (a recovery tax in other words) of 55 per cent when you take the benefits if you take the excess in a lump sum; if it is used to buy a pension, 25 per cent tax will be charged in addition to your normal income tax rate when you take your retirement income. You can register to protect those benefits (see page 49). If you stop contributing to your fund before A-Day, the fund will be exempt from the recovery tax, although you will still have to notify the Inland Revenue that enhanced protection is being claimed.

Fund values below the figures quoted above will continue to be exempt from capital gains tax, and from income tax in the vast majority of cases.

How to value your pension funds

To obtain a fund value for personal pension schemes and money purchase pensions you should ask the insurance company or scheme manager handling your pension. But how do you value a final salary scheme?

There is a formula. A ratio of 20:1 will be applied to your anticipated pension entitlement. For example, if you have a pension of £10,000 a year, the notional value will be $20 \times £10,000$, which equals £200,000.

This valuing of all your pension schemes will also apply to existing pensions, annuities and income draw-downs (excluding your State Pension entitlement) that are already in operation on A-Day. The ratio here will be 25:1.

To estimate your pension fund value you will need to do a calculation based on adding up all the following:

- The fund size of any personal pension, stakeholder pension or company pension
- the value of any final salary pension ($\times$ 20)
- the value of annuities that are currently available ($\times$ 25)
- the value of any current draw-down facility ($\times$ 25 up to the maximum)
- the value of any final salary pension being received ($\times$ 25).

Registration

You can register your pensions valuations and benefit entitlements in order to protect your rights and you have until 5 April 2009 to do this. You should consider registering if your pension funds are worth more than £1.5 million on A-Day or if your tax-free cash entitlement prior to A-Day is more than 25 per cent of the fund value under your scheme rules.

The advantage of registering is that you will avoid the recovery charge and/or retain the extra tax-free cash entitlement.

This 'protection' will not be lost on your pre-A-Day fund value if you continue to make pension contributions after that date, although the fund value of any post-A-Day contributions will obviously not be protected.

How much can you pay into your pension scheme?

How much you can legally pay into your existing schemes to get tax relief is dealt with in Chapter 6.

After A-Day you can pay up to 100 per cent of your earnings each year into one or more pension funds, but there is a maximum limit (a cap) of £215,000 a year, or £3,600 if you are a low-earner or indeed have no earnings at all, for you can still get tax relief at basic rate even if you are not a taxpayer!

The maximum annual allowance is a combined figure for both employers and employee contributions. This maximum annual allowance gradually increases each year, rising to £255,000 in 2010–2011.

Interestingly, in the 12 months prior to retirement there is no limit at all, thus giving an opportunity to top up if you have funds available, and similarly, with your employer's contributions.

What happens if you pay in more than these limits?

In the case of your employer's contributions, a tax charge (an 'annual allowance charge') of 40 per cent will be levied on you and on excess personal payments made by you; then you will get no tax relief on any amount over the limit.

Should you register?

A quick guide as to whether you should register, and thus save a future tax liability:

Are your pension funds going to be worth more than £1.5 million on A-Day?

If the answer to this is 'Yes', register to avoid the recovery tax charge and to protect any cash-free rights. If the answer is 'No' but the tax-free lump sum is more than 25 per cent, you should register to protect that right.

Annuities

Most of the annuity legislation remains unaltered – you still have until age 75 to convert your pension fund into an annuity (in future to be called *'secure income'*) once you have taken any tax-free cash, although the income draw-down provisions (to be called *'unsecured income'* in future) remain in force up to age 75 (see pages 41–2 for annuity options and income draw-down).

Two new forms of annuity will be introduced:
1. *A limited-period annuity* (as distinct from a lifetime annuity). Under this you can use part of your fund to buy an annuity specifically for five years, with the balance effectively remaining in the pot and with income draw-down options.
2. *A value-protected annuity*
   Under this annuity, if when you die the amount paid out in income does not exceed the amount of the capital used to

purchase the annuity, then the balance is paid to the annuity holder's estate, rather than with a lifetime annuity where usually there is no value after death. The estate will, however, have to pay a tax charge of 35 per cent. These value protected benefits are not available to those over 75.

The above are in addition to existing forms of annuity that were detailed in the previous chapter.

Income draw-down

As from 6 April 2006, there will be no minimum limit and the maximum will be 120 per cent instead of 100 per cent. Income draw-down will be called *unsecured income* – just to confuse us all!

There will be a new form of income draw-down available when you reach the age of 75 called *Alternative Secured Income* (ASI). Again there will be no minimum limit and the maximum will be 70 per cent of the value of the annuity that can be purchased at age 75; make sure you get several quotes. Note also that the opportunity for provision of death benefits for your partner or dependants is withdrawn.

Continue to bear in mind, however, that income draw down is depleting the capital value of your fund all the time.

Small pension funds

From 6 April 2006 if your pension fund value is £15,000 or less then you can take it as a lump sum (i.e. you do not have to buy an annuity).

Death benefits from your pension funds

There are no major changes to death benefits in the new legislation, except that the value of any death benefit might attract a recovery tax charge if the 'Lifetime Limit' of your pension funds is exceeded (as explained above).

If you die before retirement, the pension fund up to the Lifetime Limit will be paid to your estate without any tax charge, any lump sum excess being taxable at the recovery tax charge of 55 per cent and any pension provided to dependants out of that excess being subject to income tax if the dependant is a taxpayer.

On death after retirement, it will depend on the options that you decided upon when you actually retired as to the tax treatment.

As already mentioned, you may have secured an ongoing annuity for your partner, in which case that will be taxed at their personal tax rate depending on their total income level. Any Value Protection Benefits payable before age 75 will be taxed at 35 per cent.

If you had elected for income draw-down, your dependants have several avenues to explore, and these need to be discussed with your pensions adviser – normally the options will either be to purchase an annuity with the remaining cash in the total fund, which will incur a tax charge of 35 per cent, or continue the income stream under income draw-down. If the pension holder who has died is over 75, there is no lump sum option – only annuity purchase for the benefit of a surviving partner or children under the age of 23, or continuing the draw-down income under the ASI rules as mentioned above.

If there are no dependants, any fund balance is paid into a nominated charity or if applicable into the fund of another member of the pension scheme (i.e. into a family SIPP – Self Invested Personal Pension, see page 37).

What other post-6 April 2006 changes are there?

It is outside the scope of this book to deal with other areas of pension funding, but the new legislation has considerably broadened the types of investment in which pension schemes can invest, including residential property. However, it is important to consult financial advisers to ensure that you don't inadvertently incur a tax charge under the extended tax avoidance legislation on private benefits, etc.

Professional advice

Although the purpose of the new pension legislation is to simplify the existing, complicated system, the transitionary arrangements will necessitate your reassessing your pension needs, and checking the values of all past and present schemes.

In a book such as this, the pensions scene has been covered to try to signal pitfalls and assist in planning, but mainly from the standpoint of identifying the tax angles. Necessarily, only a brief coverage of the new pension legislation has been attempted, and it is important that you seek advice from an independent pensions adviser.

CHAPTER 8

Pension Credits and other tax credits

Over the past two or three years there has been a trend in the Government's thinking which has resulted in a much closer relationship between the tax system and the social security benefit system.

This started in 2001 with the introduction of Children's Tax Credit, which replaced the married couple's allowance (except for those born before 6 April 1935), the additional personal allowance, widow's bereavement allowance and relief for most maintenance payments which were all abolished from April 2000.

There were also new tax credits called the Working Families' Tax Credit and the Disabled Persons' Tax Credit. In retrospect the introduction of these tax credits, although perhaps laudable in an endeavour to increase the income of the lower paid on a means-tested basis, was very badly implemented and unnecessarily complicated which meant that lots of people were either overpaid or didn't bother to claim at all.

Pension Credit

The main tax credit with which readers will need to be familiar is the *Pension Credit*, which was introduced in October 2003 and which now incorporates the Minimum Income Guarantee. It is means-tested and is designed to top up the incomes of those people resident in the UK with low income levels and at the same time reward (slightly) those pensioners who have saved for their retirement.

As from 6 April 2005 you can claim if your weekly income is less than £109.45 for a single person and £167.05 for a couple. The credit will top up your income to at least these levels.

The term 'weekly income' is not as straightforward as it seems. Some types of income are excluded, and there are allowances for certain housing costs. The minimum income figures mentioned above are also higher if you are severely disabled, or you have a carer.

The Pension Credit consists of **two parts** – a **guarantee credit** and a **savings credit**. You must be at least 60 years of age to get the guarantee credit and at least 65 to get the savings credit. You may be entitled to the guarantee credit, or the savings credit, or indeed both.

In this chapter the term 'couple' not only means a husband and wife but also encompasses a person with whom you live as if you are married to them. (This is the wording of The Pension Service legislation, not that of the author.) Same-sex couples will need to claim as single people but can be treated as a couple once they have entered into a statutory civil registration procedure from December 2005.

If you are a couple, your **combined** income is taken into account. For the guarantee credit, it is the age of the older partner that counts (i.e. the one who is 60 or over); for savings credit at least one of a couple must have reached the age of 65.

Remember that the fact that you may be living with your grown-up family does not mean that you cannot claim the Pension Credit – the claim is based on *your* income only. Also, the fact that you own your own home does not mean that you cannot apply.

How do I know if I can claim?

You can telephone The Pension Service (which is part of the Department for Work and Pensions) on freephone 0800 99 1234 (Northern Ireland 0808 601 8821) – they are open from 8am to 8pm Monday to Friday and from 9am to 1pm on Saturdays, and they will fill in the claim form for you over the telephone and tell you if you are eligible. If you have speech or hearing difficulties, the textphone number is 0800 169 0133.

You should have your National Insurance number to hand, plus details of any pensions and other income you receive and details of any savings accounts. The form will then be sent back to you to check the details and for you to sign and return. If you would prefer to fill in the form yourself, they will send you a form to complete plus an explanatory booklet.

Note that there is also The Pension Service web site on www.thepensionservice.gov.uk (Northern Ireland www.dhssni.gov.uk), which gives further information plus a 'do-it-yourself' calculator.

If you have forgotten to claim the Pension Credit to which you were entitled, it can be backdated for up to 12 months. It is not taxable.

You have to actually claim the Pension Credit – it is not paid to you automatically. You do not have to be in work and you do not need to have paid National Insurance contributions to be entitled to the credit.

The Pension Credit will be paid to you weekly in advance, directly into your bank, building society or post office account. If you find it difficult either mentally or physically to manage one of these accounts, you can apply for it to be paid by cheque.

How do I know if it has been calculated correctly?

There will be some notes attached to the claim form which will give some guidance, but if you want to work it out yourself, or you want to check the figures once you get back the completed form, then the next section shows you how you go about doing the calculations. You may also want to do the calculations on behalf of a friend or relative to see if they can claim.

How to do the calculations

The guarantee credit: The amount of credit you are paid is the difference between what is called the 'appropriate minimum guarantee' (officially called the 'appropriate amount') and your actual income, after allowing for various deductions and taking into account your personal circumstances.

How to calculate the *appropriate amount*: It will be made up of at least four parts:

(1) The standard weekly amount. From 6 April 2005 this is £109.45 for a single person and £167.05 for a couple.

(2) An additional amount for severe disability (termed 'severe disability premium' for Housing and Council Tax Benefit). From 6 April 2005 the amounts are £45.50 for a single person (or one partner qualifying) and £91.00 for a couple, where both qualify. There are inevitably various rules and stipulations depending on whether you receive Attendance Allowance, or you live alone, and whether you receive the Carer's Allowance. Telephone the helpline on 0808 800 6565 (Northern Ireland 0808 808 7575) to check over your personal circumstances.

(3) An additional amount for carers. The amount for a single person is £25.80; for one person qualifying out of a couple, £25.80; a couple both qualifying, £51.60. Again, check with The Pension Service (as above) to see if you qualify, as there may be repercussions with any social security Carer's Allowance.

(4) An amount to defray housing costs may also be added into the guarantee credit.

This could include basic mortgage interest (not the capital repayment element) and this is limited to a loan not exceeding £100,000; interest on a loan for house repairs or improvements;

ground rent or feu duty, and certain service charges. Any additional amount claimed towards housing costs may be restricted if you have another person (other than your partner or a dependent child) living with you.

The interest rate used has been set by the Government each year but for 2005–2006 it is to be referenced to the Bank of England base rate – the actual interest that you pay is not used.

So, to summarise, adding all or any of the above options together will give the 'appropriate amount'. Call it AA for convenience.

Now calculate your total income

Compile a list of your income after taking into account any tax or National Insurance deductions, however, you can specifically *exclude* from your total income:
- Attendance Allowance
- Disability Living Allowance
- Housing Benefit
- Council Tax Benefit
- Bereavement payments
- Child Benefit
- Any payment from the Social Fund
- War Widow's Pension (pre-1973 legislation).

You can also ignore any expenses reimbursed by an employer, any gifts in kind, most charitable and voluntary payments and annuities received for gallantry awards, and any payments from friends, family, etc. are also ignored.

Any interest you receive from your savings can be ignored at this stage – *but* see below if your savings capital is above £6,000. You do not have to include the Government payments that are not means-tested and are received (or should be received) by all pensioners (i.e. Winter Fuel Payment, council tax contribution, Christmas Bonus).

What about a home income plan such as a mortgage annuity, home reversion scheme or roll-up loan? You must include any net weekly income you receive but you can ignore the interest element that might be applicable to any loan taken out for this purpose. If the plan gave you a capital sum, then any unspent amount is included in the savings amount mentioned above.

Just to add a further complication, you are allowed to exclude from your total income the first £5 of any earnings if you work and are single (£10 in the case of a couple, even if only one partner is earning) and the first £10 of a War Widow's/Widower's Pension or War Disablement Pension.

There are also amounts you can deduct from earnings if you are a carer, or receiving rent from a sub-tenant or boarder (telephone 0800 99 1234 to check your entitlement).

Once you have totalled your income, as defined above, pause a while to consider your savings if they are over the maximum capital amount of £6,000.

What are savings?

They include cash, bank balances, building society accounts, investments (valued at the market rate on the day you claim) and National Savings products (current cash-in value). You do not have to include the value of the house you own and live in or your personal possessions, pensions or annuity funds. Instead of the actual income you receive from your savings you substitute £1 of income for every £500 (or part of £500) of savings over the maximum capital amount. For example, if you had savings of, say, £14,800, then £14,800 − £6,000 = £8,800 and, at £1 for every £500, this equals £18 of income *a week*.

Incidentally, the maximum capital amount if you live permanently in a care home is £10,000 instead of £6,000. (If you are a couple, you must add your savings together but the maximum amounts are the same as for a single person − as above.) Having done the savings calculation, then that is the extra weekly income you have to add on to your total income figure.

You have now calculated your net weekly income. Call it WI for convenience.

Summary
If your weekly income (WI) is less than the appropriate amount (AA), you are entitled to claim Pension Credit.

It may be useful to show a few examples of how these calculations of the guarantee credit might appear in practice, to help clarify things.

Example 1
Betty, aged 63, lives with her married son and only receives the State Pension of £82.05 a week.
As her weekly income is less than her appropriate amount (AA) − see page 55 − of £109.45, she can claim the difference of £27.40 as guarantee credit.

Example 2

Roy, aged 64, has part-time earnings of £87.20 a week and a weekly pension from his former employer of £20.50.

His total income is therefore £107.70 (WI).

His appropriate amount (i.e. the Pension Credit applicable to his circumstances) is £109.45. As his WI is less than the appropriate amount (AA) he can claim the difference of £1.75 as guarantee credit.

If he had savings of, say, £8,000, his weekly income would have been £107.70 plus £1 for each £500 over £6,000 (i.e. £4), making a total of £111.70. Then his total income would be more than his appropriate amount and he would not be entitled to Pension Credit until after his 65th birthday, when he could claim savings credit.

Example 3

Bob, aged 66, is severely disabled and has savings of under £6,000.

		£
His total weekly income is:	State Pension	82.05
	Occupational pension	60.00
	WI	142.05
His appropriate amount is:	standard amount	109.45
	severe disability	45.50
	AA	154.95

As his WI is less than AA, he can claim the difference of £12.90 as Pension Credit; he may also claim savings credit.

How to calculate the savings credit

The savings credit: If you are 65 or over, you may get the savings part of the Pension Credit. You may get it on its own even if you do not qualify for the guarantee credit mentioned above – or you may get some savings credit paid on top of the guarantee credit.

If you are married, only one of you has to be aged 65 or over to claim the savings credit. To calculate how much savings credit you can claim is not easy – and it certainly bears out the author's view that the Government seem intent on making it very difficult for you to check the Pension Credit calculations; but a lot of pensioners are not getting their full entitlement, which is why this chapter is necessarily lengthy in order to try to break down the process into as simple a form as possible.

As with the guarantee credit referred to above, you have to make a note of your total net income but this time you can exclude:

- Working Tax Credit
- Incapacity Benefit
- Jobseeker's Allowance
- Severe Disablement Allowance
- Maternity Allowance
- Maintenance payments from a spouse or former spouse.

This is called your weekly *qualifying* income (WQI).

Whether you can claim savings credit and, if so, how much, is governed by:

(a) Your appropriate amount (see page 55) AA
(b) Your net weekly income (see page 57) WI
(c) Your qualifying income (see above) WQI
(d) The savings credit starting point as from 6 April 2005 is £82.05 for a single person and £131.20 for a couple
(e) The maximum amount of savings credit that anyone can receive is £16.44 for a single person and £21.51 for a couple.

Savings credit – the final calculations

This is the simplest way (believe it or not!):

- If your weekly qualifying income (WQI) is the same or less than the savings credit starting point, you cannot get savings credit.
- If your weekly qualifying income is more than the savings credit starting point, you *may* be entitled to a savings credit, and you need to do the following calculation.

If your net weekly income (WI) is less than or the same as your appropriate amount (AA), your savings credit will be 60 per cent of the difference between your WQI and the savings credit starting point up to a maximum of £16.44 for a single person and £21.51 for a couple. Call this 'Amount A'.

If, however, your weekly income (WI) is *more* than the appropriate amount, calculate 'Amount B' (which is 40 per cent of the difference between WI and AA) and deduct this Amount B from Amount A, and what is left is the amount of savings credit you can claim.

There follows some examples to help smooth the way!

Example 4

Joan is 63 and widowed. Her savings are less than £6,000. She has the following total weekly income:

	£
State Pension	82.05
Occupational pension	12.00
Total income (WI)	94.05

Her appropriate amount for a single person is £109.45.

Therefore, she gets a guaranteed credit of £109.45 less £94.05 which equals £15.40 a week.

She is not entitled to savings credit as she is under 65.

How would the situation have changed if Joan had been aged 65 or over?

Her guarantee credit would stay the same.

Her qualifying income, £94.05 (which happens to be the same as her total income), is above the savings credit starting point of £82.05, therefore she can get savings credit of:

	£
Qualifying income	94.05
Less: savings credit starting point	82.05
	12.00
× 60% =	£7.20

This is less than the maximum income limit of £16.44, so Joan gets £7.20 as savings credit to add to her guarantee credit above of £15.40, giving her a total weekly Pension Credit of £22.60.

Example 5

Peter is 66. He is single with a State Pension of £104.00. His savings are £7,200, he owns his own flat, with no mortgage, and pays ground rent of £10 a week.

His weekly income is therefore:

	£
State Pension	104.00
Savings: £1 for each £500 over £6,000	3.00
	107.00
His appropriate amount is	109.45
Ground rent	10.00
	119.45

His guarantee credit will be £119.45 less £107.00, which equals £12.45.

As he is over 65, he can consider claiming the savings credit.

His weekly qualifying income is less than the appropriate amount, therefore his savings credit will be £107.00 less the savings credit starting point £82.05 = £24.95 × 60% = £14.97.

His total Pension Credit will therefore be £12.45 plus £14.97 = £27.42.

Example 6

Chris and Sue are married and both are aged 71. Their combined weekly total income is a State Pension of £131.20 and an occupational pension of £36.00. They live in their own home with no mortgage and have savings of £15,000.

Their total income is therefore:

	£
State Pension	131.20
Occupational pension	36.00
	167.20
Savings: £15,000 – £6,000 =	
£9,000 at £1 for every £500	18.00
	185.20

Their appropriate amount for a couple with no special additions is £167.05.

As their income is higher than their appropriate amount, they are not entitled to guarantee credit.

They could, however, see if they are entitled to savings credit as follows.

As their weekly income is more than their appropriate amount:

The difference between qualifying income of £185.20 and the appropriate amount of £167.05 = £18.15 $\times$ 40% = £7.26.

Deduct £7.26 from the maximum savings credit of £21.51, which means they can claim a savings credit of £14.25 a week.

It's an incredible equation to work through and it's quite unbelievable that anyone could have conceived such convoluted calculations, but that's the law as it stands today!

Telephone the Pension Credit line on 0800 99 1234 for help and advice – don't be surprised if it's engaged! Or try the Help the Aged senior line on 0808 800 6565 (Northern Ireland 0808 808 7575).

Reassessment

You will be glad to know that you don't have to go through the above rigmarole every year. Your income level is assessed at retirement and then reassessed every five years, unless there are major changes in your circumstances in between times, when it is up to you to advise The Pension Service and request a reassessment. Bear in mind you may have to repay any sums paid to you if it transpires that your circumstances had changed materially and you did not advise them.

When you first get your Pension Credit, you will be advised what changes in circumstances you have to report.

Child Tax Credit

Anyone can claim the Child Tax Credit regardless of their age if they are responsible for looking after and caring for a child under the age of 16, or under 18 if he or she is receiving full-time education.

There are many pensioners who are in this position, and it's important that they claim not only the Child Tax Credit but also the Child Benefit, which is payable monthly directly into the carer's bank account. (Child Benefit is tax free; it is not means-tested and does not have to be declared in your tax return.)

To claim the Child Tax Credit, telephone 0800 500 2220 or visit the web site www.hmrc.gov.uk. The chart reproduced in Appendix 2 gives a very broad guideline only and is issued by the Inland Revenue. It shows you the income limits and the corresponding amount of Child Tax Credit you may expect to receive.

The amount you receive will depend on a number of factors – how many children you are caring for, and the age of each child. Additional sums are also claimable for a disabled worker or disabled child, a child under one year old or someone aged 50 or over returning to work after a period of unemployment.

Is it means-tested?

Yes it is, but you can have joint income up to £58,000 a year (and up to £66,000 a year if you have a child under one year old) before you lose the benefit, so the earnings levels are quite generous. The Child Tax Credit is not taxable.

What income is considered?

If you are single (or separated), your claim will be based on your total income; if you are a married couple, or a man and a woman living together as if you are married, your combined total income will be taken into account.

Total income is considered to include earnings from employment or self-employment, some social security benefits, income from savings and investments including rents (but excluding Rent-a-Room income). You are, however, allowed to deduct payments into a pension scheme and donations to Gift Aid.

If your circumstances change

When the Child Tax Credit started, applicants' incomes were based on their earnings for the tax year 2001–2002. From 6 April 2004 the previous year's income level (2003–2004) was taken into account and likewise the income levels for 2004–2005 will be used for assessing any 2005 entitlement. Therefore if a change occurs – for example, your earnings take you into a higher band, you have further child responsibilities or you change jobs – you may want to notify the Inland Revenue as soon as possible, either by filling in form TC602 (which would have been sent to you when you first registered for Child Tax Credit) or by telephoning the helpline, 0845 300 3900 (0845 603 2000 in Northern Ireland). Otherwise you can wait until the end of the year and your entitlement will then be revised although additional income of up to £2,500 will be disregarded. You are, however, obliged to report certain changes in your circumstances – such as marital status or child care payments – within three months, or penalties may be imposed.

Claims for tax credit will only be backdated for three months, so if you are self-employed and your accounts will not be completed soon enough to determine your eligibility within three months of the tax year start, it is worth putting in a protective claim.

For further information, telephone the claim line on 0800 500 2220.

In addition to the Child Tax Credit, you may also be eligible for the Working Tax Credit.

Working Tax Credit (WTC)

This is a payment to top up the earnings of those who are in low-income employment, including workers who do not have children. The amount you will receive will depend on your income level, the number of hours you work, your age, whether you have any children for whom you are caring, whether you are disabled and whether you are involved in paying for child care to a registered provider. The calculation is very complicated but Appendix 2 gives a broad idea of likely benefit levels.

If you are employed, the WTC is paid to you by your employer through the PAYE tax system; any child care element is paid directly to the person responsible for paying for that care. If you are self-employed, any WTC claim will be paid to you directly.

The telephone helpline, claim line and web site for more information are the same as for the Child Tax Credit above.

As with the Child Tax Credit you must keep the Inland Revenue informed of any change in circumstances, otherwise either you will not get all the tax credit to which you are entitled or you may have to repay sums where you have claimed too much. The Working Tax Credit is not taxable.

Other benefits

Do always remember that in addition to the tax credits and benefits mentioned above, your local council or social security office will also advise you on other benefits you can claim – for example Income Support, Housing Benefit, Funeral Payment, Social Fund Payment, Council Tax Benefit, budgeting loans and Cold Weather Payment, to name but a few.

Jobseeker's Allowance for people under pension age

Jobseeker's Allowance can be claimed by those that are unemployed, and it is taxable. There are two parts – firstly, an allowance based on your National Insurance contributions paid (or credited) to date; and, secondly, an allowance which is income-based and therefore means-tested.

To qualify you must be under pensionable age (those above should consider Pension Credit instead), unemployed or working for less than 16 hours a week, capable of work and actively seeking work.

Where to claim? Contact your local Jobcentre Plus office.

CHAPTER 9

Savings and tax

It is probably true to say that most men and women born in the second and third quarters of the nineteen-hundreds had instilled into them by their parents that it was a sensible and prudent thing to build up savings as a cushion for later in life.

Although that is as true today as it was then, there has been a significant shift in the attitude to savings, brought about by the changes in the taxation system and, more importantly, the social security system.

There is a tendency now to penalise elderly pensioners if they have savings. For example, many of the means-tested social security benefits get reduced if you have savings, and your options if you have to sell your house and go into State care can be greatly affected, by virtue of your savings level.

Are you a taxpayer?

This question has been asked many times throughout this book (see in particular Chapter 2) because it is so important. If your total income exceeds your tax allowances, then you are a taxpayer, although you might not necessarily be paying tax at the basic rate of 22 per cent. This is because the first £2,090 of your income (after allowances) is taxed at 10 per cent before going on to the basic-rate band. These rates are for 2005–2006 and the income limits are usually increased in each year's Spring Budget.

There are five important issues to consider when deciding where to invest your savings:

- Make sure that you have some savings where you can get at your money quickly in an emergency.
- Make sure you are making full use of tax-free savings.
- Make sure that you are not putting money into taxable investments where you are unable to reclaim, or offset, any tax deducted.
- Make sure that you are not limiting social security benefits by getting income from investments.
- Make sure that you are not taking unnecessary risks or, at least if you are, do ensure that you understand the full repercussions if things go wrong.

Various savings opportunities and their tax implications are now considered below.

Emergency savings

There is no point in putting money into a good investment if you cannot get your money out quickly, or where there are penalties for early withdrawal. Interest may be relatively low with some of the more boring savings vehicles like National Savings accounts, bank or building society deposits – and even no interest at all like Premium Bonds – but at least you can get your cash out quickly and without risk.

Tax-free savings

Individual savings accounts (ISAs)

All income and capital gains are free of tax from these accounts and since their introduction in 1999 the range of savings accounts has blossomed materially. Until 5 April 2004 there was a concession on dividends whereby ISA fund managers could reclaim the 10 per cent dividend credit; this facility was abolished from 5 April 2004, and has also meant that investors in an equity ISA are not now able to reclaim the 10 per cent tax rate. Investors in bonds that are wrapped around an ISA, however, will still be able to reclaim the tax paid on income because bond income is considered to be interest rather than dividends, so the tax credit remains at 20 per cent and claimable.

The maximum investment each year is £7,000. You can split your investment into cash deposits (like a bank deposit account), life insurance and stocks and shares but there are maximum limits for each form of investment. The annual limit for cash is £3,000, and for life insurance products it is £1,000. There is no individual limit for stocks and shares other than that the total must not exceed £7,000. Why the Government have to set these individual limits is hard to imagine – it only adds confusion and creates even more paperwork and checking. Husbands and wives each have their own limits.

There is no penalty for early encashment except that, if you do subscribe the maximum amount in a year and then withdraw sums, you will not be allowed to replenish the account until the start of the next tax year.

Just to add a further confusion, there are two types of ISA: maxi and mini! Under a *maxi*, savers can spread their money between cash deposits, life products and shares in a single plan run by an insurance company. With a *mini*, you can have a separate financial service provider for each category, but you cannot have a mix of minis and maxis in the same year!

There is a helpline, 0845 604 1701. You do not have to declare ISAs in your tax return.

TESSA-only ISAs (also known as TOISA accounts)

TESSA tax-free savings accounts ceased as from 6 April 1999, but if you held a TESSA at that date then within six months of maturity you could transfer the proceeds into a TOISA account and that would not count toward your annual ISA investment limit (see above). So you could end up holding both of these tax-efficient savings plans.

Personal equity plans (PEPs)

PEPs are tax-free savings plans that were abolished in 1999, but if you still held one at 5 April 1999 then you are still entitled to the tax benefits (tax-free dividend income and no capital gains tax on the proceeds) and can transfer your plan to another PEP provider; but do check the charges carefully before you do so.

Friendly societies

With friendly societies, you have to invest for a period of ten years as a minimum, and the maximum you can invest each year is only £270. Interest is tax free but charges can be rather high and there are penalties for early encashment.

Where to put your savings if you are not a taxpayer

It's sensible to put your money into investments that pay interest gross, that is, without tax having been deducted; that way you will not have the hassle of reclaiming the tax back and you will benefit from an improved cash flow. Therefore, consider the following, all of which pay interest gross and are short-term safe investments.

Building society and bank deposit or savings accounts

If you are not a taxpayer, when you open your account (or, indeed, if you become a non-taxpayer after you have opened an account), ask your bank or building society for a form R85 or download the form from the Inland Revenue web site. It's a very simple form and on it you confirm that your income is below the taxable limit.

You will need your National Insurance number. Sign the form and return it to the bank or building society, and that will be their confirmation that they can pay you interest without deducting tax.

Remember, however, that if at any time your total income exceeds your tax allowances then you must tell your bank or building society and they will then start deducting tax from the interest.

If you do not complete the above form, tax at the savings rate will be deducted. At the end of the year, when you check your income and the tax you have suffered, if you have overpaid then you have to reclaim it (see Chapter 3). You must declare the interest in any tax return that you fill in.

What about windfalls? A cash windfall on a building society takeover/conversion is liable to capital gains tax but remember that you can make capital profits of £8,500 in 2005–2006 before you have to pay capital gains tax. In the case of a cash windfall on a merger, this is treated in the same way as interest and must be declared on your tax return. You could also consider offshore accounts (see page 71).

National Savings generally
National Savings have a telephone enquiry line on 0845 964 5000 and a web site at www.nsandi.com on which you can see current rates and a product listing.

National Savings bonds
With *income bonds* you can receive regular monthly payments of interest while preserving the full cash value of the investment. With *capital and fixed-rate bonds*, interest is calculated gross and added to the capital value annually. The interest must be declared on your tax return. Any capital appreciation is free of tax.

National Savings bank accounts
The first £70 of interest earned on the ordinary account is tax free; any excess above this you must include in your tax return. However, since July 2004 no one has been able to open a new ordinary account – these were replaced with easy access accounts (see below). Ordinary accounts will remain dormant until they are either closed by the saver or are transferred to a new easy access account.

A National Savings *investment* account pays a slightly higher interest rate. The interest is credited to your account every 31 December. The tax office will accept this figure to go in your tax return; you do not have to apportion it over a time basis.

National Savings easy access account
Easy access accounts pay a variable rate of interest depending on the amount of money in the account. Interest is paid gross and added to your account on 31 March each year. The rate of interest on amounts over £1,000 is higher than the investment account mentioned above. The full amount of interest must be declared on your tax return; there is no exemption.

Pensioners' guaranteed income bonds
There are one, two or five-year bonds available. They all carry a fixed rate of interest and are specifically for people over 60 years of age.

You must have a bank, building society or National Savings account to which interest can be transferred automatically. If you want to obtain early repayment, 60 days' notice is required, with a corresponding loss of income.

Obviously there is no risk as regards your capital but if you invest in fixed-interest bonds then you will lose out if interest rates increase materially.

Make a note of the maturity date in your diary. Although the National Savings office will write to you if you don't respond within a couple of weeks, they will automatically reinvest your capital in a similarly dated bond and you will lose your option to make a choice. The interest should be declared on your tax return.

Premium Bonds

These are not strictly an investment – more a gamble. But at least your capital is safe and erosion by inflation might be offset by a winning number.

Another point to bear in mind, perhaps, is that the numbers stay in the draw for up to 12 months after death, with any winnings being paid to your estate and at the first anniversary after death the bonds' capital value will be paid to your estate, unless of course the executors have cashed the bonds in earlier.

Government stocks (gilt-edged securities)

These can be purchased from the Bank of England Registrar. Telephone 0800 818 614 for a form. The interest is paid to you regularly without tax having been deducted, but you can request that tax be deducted if you wish. Any capital gain is tax free but the interest should be declared on your tax return. The interest is subject to the accrued income scheme; the rules are complicated but ensure, for instance, that you are taxed on the daily interest accrued if you sell before a security becomes 'ex dividend'.

Other investment considerations

Index-linked National Savings Certificates

You do not receive interest but if you hold them for at least one year your capital is inflation-proofed, with annual supplements expanded to 3 per cent compound interest over a two or five year period (you can choose which period when you buy them); this capital appreciation is exempt from income tax and capital gains tax and does not have to be shown in your tax return.

offer high interest rates but where capital repayment is geared to the performance of a Stock Exchange index or bundle of indices. Many investors in these have lost a large percentage of their initial investment over the last year or two, and the Financial Ombudsman Service has been inundated by complaints of mis-selling.

Shares quoted on the Stock Exchange

You will have seen this warning on numerous adverts: 'Shares can go down as well as up' – so make sure you bear this in mind when considering investing in company shares, and make sure that you have first made provision for 'rainy day' savings before you attempt the more risky strategy of investing in shares.

Dividends are paid after allowing for a tax credit of 10 per cent *which you cannot reclaim if you are a non-taxpayer*. This was the very major change in the Budget of 1997 which meant that pension funds could not reclaim their tax credits. This resulted in a significant reduction in the value of almost everyone's pension fund.

The amount of dividend received plus the tax credit have to be shown in your tax return and included in your total income in calculating your overall tax liability. If this takes you into the higher-rate tax band then more tax will have to be paid. If you are a basic-rate taxpayer there is no further tax liability.

Enterprise Investment Schemes (EISs)

Under an EIS an individual can gain very significant tax relief by investing in unquoted trading companies. There are now many such investment opportunities on offer. The rules and regulations governing these schemes are very complex so do seek professional advice before investing.

The main provisions are:

- Income tax relief is given at 20 per cent on qualifying investments up to £200,000 in any tax year.
- Gains on disposal are exempt from capital gains tax.
- There is income tax relief or capital gains tax relief for losses on disposal.
- Eligible shares must be held for at least three years if issued after 6 April 2000 (five years for investments earlier than this) so do bear in mind that if you sell prematurely you will lose the tax benefits.
- Any amount invested in the first six months of a tax year (6 April to 5 October) can be carried back to the previous tax year up to a maximum of £25,000.

- Any chargeable gain you have on any other investments can be reinvested in an EIS to obtain a deferral of capital gains tax, provided you make such EIS investment between one and three years after the disposal date of the investment that produced the gain.
- For eligible shares on or after 6 April 1998, the subscription must be wholly in cash.
- Certain EIS investments (AIM trading companies, see below) will be free from inheritance tax if held for at least two years, as they will count as business assets.

Venture Capital Trusts (VCTs)
How do VCTs differ from Enterprise Investment Schemes? Basically these trusts are a basket of various EISs so that by investing in a VCT you are spreading your risk – rather like investing in an investment trust which has a portfolio of very many different companies.

VCT shares are quoted on the alternative investment market (AIM – the stock market for small and young companies) or traded on Ofex (the off-exchange trading facility for even smaller companies) which helps as regards flexibility in being able to sell when you want to. As VCTs invest in newly issued shares in small- and medium-sized companies, so an element of risk is still present. However, this can be restricted if you pick VCTs that state clearly that they will buy back shares if they fall below a specific level compared with the company's net asset value.

Rather like EISs you get 40 per cent tax relief on an investment of up to £200,000 a year (20 per cent and £100,000 prior to April 2004) if held for three years (five years prior to 6 April 2000). Individuals are exempt from tax on dividends and capital gains tax although losses cannot be offset against other non-VCT gains. As with EISs your capital investment in a VCT can be used to defer a capital gain (as above) but the time span is more restrictive: gains must arise within 12 months prior to or 12 months after your VCT purchase. Remember that if you sell your VCT shares within three years you will have to pay back all the tax reliefs received. You claim tax relief by filling in the VCT section of your tax return (Q15).

Investing in a property
Investing in a second property other than your own home has reaped good rewards over the past few years, with spiralling house prices. Whether this will continue is anyone's guess. Remember that you will be liable for income tax on the rental income after deducting expenses and mortgage interest if applicable, and you will also be liable for

capital gains tax on any capital profit when you sell. You have to declare these income and expenses in the Land and Property supplementary pages of your tax return.

Company profit-sharing schemes

If you were working for a company that provided shares under a profit-sharing scheme, there are usually options for you to put those shares into a stakeholder pension or an ISA (individual savings account).

Do you have an endowment policy?

Many people took out this form of insurance policy, often to 'cover' a possible contingency like paying off a mortgage or celebrating early retirement, but often the policy was not cashed in but continues to exist after its original purpose has perhaps become obsolete.

There is a sound financial market now for selling on these policies and you should get quotations from a professional adviser – contact the Association of Market Makers. Financially, it is usually best to hold on to a policy until maturity, especially if you are getting tax relief which is available only to pre-14 March 1984 policies.

Giving to grandchildren in a tax-efficient way?

Child Trust Fund

As from April 2005 the Government started a new savings vehicle called the Child Trust Fund. This will apply for each baby born after 1 September 2002, and the Government will contribute between £250 and £500 depending on family income levels. So far, so good; but the interesting bit comes in the fact that anyone else can contribute to each child's trust fund. So, as grandparents – or indeed parents or just friends – you can add up to £1,200 a year to the trust. The fund becomes the child's property when they reach the age of 18, to spend as they want. There can be no withdrawals prior to that age.

The tax advantages are that all income earned in the fund will be free of income tax and capital gains tax. The Government have further announced that when a child is seven they will contribute a further sum into each trust – the amount has yet to be announced.

There is no specific tax advantage as far as the giver is concerned and contributions do not have to be mentioned in your tax return. For further information go to www.childtrustfund.gov.uk or call the helpline on 0845 302 1470.

Other savings accounts

As grandparents (but not as parents) you can gift sums of money into a savings account set up in the name of a child – remember that children have their own personal tax allowance for income tax (and indeed capital gains tax) so they will not pay tax on savings until their tax-free levels are exhausted. Children cannot open an ISA account until they are 16 years of age and it is not a good idea to set up an ISA in the child's parent's name as that will impinge on their ISA allowance.

CHAPTER 10

Your family home

In the chapter on inheritance tax, mention is made of the fact that your home could well be your most valuable asset and, with seemingly ever-increasing property values in the UK, it is the value of your house that may well be taking you into the inheritance tax bracket. In that chapter (Chapter 15) various schemes are outlined to try to mitigate that unjust tax.

However, there will be many people who are not so much concerned with the problems of inheritance tax but more concerned with getting over the financial hurdles of day-to-day living.

There are thousands of people who, as they get older, have very limited income but are sitting on a veritable gold mine in the capital of their house, for the price of the average house has at least doubled in the last decade.

So, a situation exists where a person, or couple, appear fairly well off on paper, but in terms of income to pay for everyday living expenses they could be struggling. This is where equity release schemes come into play.

Equity release schemes

There are three types: home reversion schemes applicable perhaps to those aged over 65; lifetime mortgages for those in their mid-fifties and above; and home income plans. Even if you have an existing mortgage, some scheme providers will still quote for an equity release scheme.

Home reversion schemes

Under these schemes, which are more popular with older home-owners, you sell your home, or a part of it, to a specialist company who pay you a discounted price as a lump sum or in staged payments so that you have capital on which to live.

You obviously continue to live in the house and you remain liable for ongoing maintenance, repairs, insurance, council tax, etc. As regards repairs, bear in mind that as the loan company have a vested interest in the condition of your property, to protect their ongoing investment and ultimately maximise their return, you could be under fairly stringent obligations to keep the property in tiptop condition.

When you die (or wish to move out), the property is sold and the specialist company will get their share of the proceeds according to the percentage share they purchased. They will thus benefit from the capital appreciation, for don't forget that they originally purchased their share at a discounted price, sometimes up to a third less than the market value.

There are many variations on this theme and there are numerous companies selling this form of reversion scheme.

Here are seven basic factors that you should consider:

1. Approach various companies for quotations so that you can compare figures, and ensure that the company is a member of the Safe Home Income Plans (SHIP) Association. Members of this self-regulating association agree to abide by an acceptable code of conduct.
2. Use an independent solicitor to handle the transaction, not the solicitor suggested by the home reversion company.
3. Ensure that the agreement allows you to move to another property if you wish, with the option of transferring the scheme to the new house.
4. Clarify that the agreement is only terminated on the death of the last marriage partner and that you can stay in your house until you die.
5. Use an independent financial adviser, not one that is beholden to one particular reversion company.
6. Make sure you get in writing a statement detailing all costs and any penalties that might be incurred if your circumstances change.
7. Check that the scheme has a guaranteed sum if you die shortly after taking out the plan.

Beware also that giving up a slice of security in your home means you have far less to pass over to your family; on the other hand, this could be of some benefit if you face possible inheritance tax liabilities.

At the moment these schemes do not have the financial protection provided by the financial services regulations, but the legislation is expected to cover these schemes within the next year or two.

There should be no hidden tax problems with this type of reversion scheme, and tax will only rear its ugly head if you invest some of your new-found capital in income-producing investments which are not tax free (see Chapter 9).

Lifetime mortgages

Interest roll-up mortgages

These schemes enable you to mortgage your house to a company who will lend you an agreed percentage of the value; you either get a lump sum of money, or individual loans spread out over a period. Unlike a normal mortgage, however, you do not actually pay interest nor make loan repayments of capital on the amount you have borrowed. Instead the interest is added to the loan and 'rolled up'.

When the time comes to sell the house (because you want to move elsewhere or go into long-term care, or you die), the mortgage company get repayment of their loan, and of course the interest which will have been accumulating over perhaps many years.

There are schemes which offer a fixed interest rate so at least you know exactly what your theoretical outgoings will be in advance, or a capped rate whereby your interest can fall but if national interest rates go up then your rate cannot exceed the capped amount. There are some schemes which offer variable rates, but here you will be at the mercy of outside economic factors affecting interest rates and you will have no control over the effective build-up of your debt. These are not recommended.

However, if the value of the original loan plus the accumulated interest is higher than the sale proceeds, the resultant 'loss' is down to the mortgage company – it cannot be claimed from your estate if the lender is party to the Safe Home Incomes Plan scheme. Any profit does pass to your estate.

With the build-up of capital repayments and compounded interest there may not be much value left in your house to pass on with your estate when you come to sell, although this would not be too significant a factor if you have no close beneficiaries.

Previously, these loans have not been covered by any compensation schemes or legal monitoring, so there have been instances in the past few years of some unscrupulous dealings; however, these schemes will now usually come under the regulation of the Financial Services Authority, which provide more safeguards.

Interest-only mortgages

This is a straightforward mortgage on which you only pay the interest charges, any capital repayment being frozen until your death or the eventual sale of your house. Interest can be either fixed or variable, but bear in mind that, if you elect for a variable interest rate and your income remains static, should interest rates rise significantly you could have difficulty paying the mortgage interest and may be forced to sell the property. This may be particularly pertinent when only one partner in a marriage survives, the mortgage having been taken out when both were alive and perhaps had a greater joint income.

Home income plans

These are similar to the home reversion schemes and mortgage schemes mentioned above but instead of receiving a lump sum you can elect to have the loan invested in an annuity in order to give you an ongoing stream of income. Annuities can either be at a level rate or index-linked to keep pace with inflation but obviously this latter option will cost you more. These plans are regulated by the Financial Services Authority and are thus much more reliable than the home income plans that were marketed prior to 1990, which often had variable-interest-rate loans and which were surrounded with much bad publicity when many people got into serious financial difficulties.

You will still be liable for the property outgoings (maintenance, insurance, repairs, council tax, etc.), so do take these into account in calculating your net spendable income.

Your annuity will be split between capital and income and this will be clearly stated when you sign all the documents.

When you elect for an annuity (and this can be index-linked to property values with some schemes), the income element will form part of your total income for tax purposes and as State and other benefits (e.g. Pension Credit, council tax rebates) are governed by your total income, you could lose out on some of these, so do make sure you check out all the possible repercussions.

Because of the decline in annuity rates in recent years, home income plans have become less popular, most people preferring the reversion schemes or mortgage schemes covered earlier in this chapter.

Pre-9 March 1999 home income annuity

Home income plans taken out before 9 March 1999 had special tax rules in that you could get the interest on the first £30,000 of a mortgage allowed for tax, provided at least 90 per cent of the lump sum received on mortgaging your house was used to purchase an annuity. This facility still exists for those pre-1999 mortgages, and you claim mortgage relief by filling in box 15.1 of your tax return.

Annuities and the tax position

The capital portion of your annuity is not taxable but the income portion will have tax deducted from it at the savings rate (20 per cent for 2005–2006) when it is paid to you by the annuity provider, you need to declare this income and the tax deducted on your tax return in boxes 10.12 to 10.14. The annuity provider will give you an annual certificate showing these totals. Whether you can claim back any of this tax will depend on your total income and tax allowances (see Chapter 2).

Your annuity contract may state a minimum period for which the annuity is payable (say five years) so that the income will continue to be paid to your estate even if you die within the stated period.

Remember that annuity rates for couples are usually lower than for single people because the income stream has to continue until the second person dies.

The annuity consideration is really only beneficial if you are, say, over 80 years old; otherwise the income from the annuity will be fairly low.

Recent tax scares

Badly drawn-up legislation by the Treasury has caused much confusion and has panicked many older people who had had equity release schemes to release capital (while at the same time continuing to live in their home), leading them to think that they would have a retrospective tax to pay on this benefit!

It has now been clarified in the March 2005 Budget that such a tax was not intended to apply to genuine equity release schemes through established companies, but to situations where the interest in a house has been 'passed' to a relative or children in order to avoid inheritance tax, but the owner has remained in residence rent free. This is known as pre-owned asset regulation. Even here, it has now been confirmed by the Inland Revenue that any such 'interfamily' deals prior to 6 April 2005 were not to be penalised by a tax assessment, but any home disposals between relatives or partners after 5 April 2005 will be liable for the new income tax charges unless the sale was for a consideration other than money or readily realisable assets. This is generally assumed to mean that an exemption would be applied if, for example, an adult child moved in with a parent and took on their care in exchange for part-ownership of the house (see also Chapter 15 on inheritance tax).

Rent-a-Room

A far less complicated way of getting some income from your home without selling it or entering into one of the equity release schemes, which are often complicated and worrying, is to let out a room in your home for rent. Under the Rent-a-Room scheme, the Inland Revenue allow you to have rental income of up to £4,250 a year tax free – and the rent does not form part of your total income for tax or State benefit purposes. You must live in the property yourself, it must be your main home and the accommodation must be furnished. Remember to tell your insurers and your mortgage company, if applicable, if you enter into a Rent-a-Room scheme.

If your rent from this scheme is over £4,250, you can still take advantage of the tax breaks. You can either pay tax on the excess over £4,250 or treat the whole rental exercise on a commercial basis by taking the gross rents received, deducting any allowable expenditure and paying tax on the difference between the two figures. It is usually easier and more beneficial to adopt the Rent-a-Room basis and pay tax on any excess rent.

If you are not a taxpayer (that is, your allowances exceed your income), you don't have to tell the Inland Revenue about your Rent-a-Room income; if you are a taxpayer or are asked to fill in a tax return, enter the details in question 5 on the Land and Property pages. It's all quite simple.

Incidentally, claiming Rent-a-Room relief does not make your house liable to capital gains tax (see Chapter 14).

What happens to your home if you go into care?

Financial assistance with care home fees may be available from social services via your local authority, but it will depend on the amount of capital you have. Capital includes savings, investments and property, including your home. Therefore, it is worth considering equity release schemes – perhaps to fund long-term care – as an alternative to actually selling the whole of your house. You are effectively making a decision as to whether you and your heirs get your property, or the local authority or tax man!

The value of your home will not be taken into account, however, if your partner (which includes someone who lives with you as though you were married) occupied the house; or it is occupied by a relative who is aged 60 or over (or someone younger who is incapacitated), a former partner who is divorced but who is a lone parent, or a child under 16 who you are liable to maintain.

Help with repairs and improvements

There is a charitable trust called the Home Improvement Trust which works closely with local authorities to help older home-owners release some of the capital tied up in their home in order to pay for repairs or improvements. Contact your local council or Age Concern to find your nearest branch. There is an equivalent in Scotland called Care and Repair Forum Scotland (telephone 0141 221 9879).

Enduring power of attorney

We all tend to feel that our mental faculties, if not our physical ones, will stay with us for ever; unfortunately one of the most distressing circumstances is when an older person becomes mentally incapacitated. A simple legal document called an enduring power of attorney, for preparation of which you should consult a solicitor, enables you to nominate a person to act legally on your behalf in the event that an independent medical adviser confirms that you are not able to cope on your own. It is rather like appointing an executor of your will but in this event the person may have to act on your behalf before you die. Obviously you need to appoint someone who you know well and who is trustworthy and would understand your wishes, which you will detail when you sign the document.

Council tax

Claim reduction of council tax from your local council if you have limited income and only modest savings. If you live alone, you can claim a reduction of 25 per cent. Contact your local council for a leaflet.

CHAPTER 11

Living abroad – your pension and tax position

If you move abroad to work before you retire, then depending on your destination country, you may be able to continue within the UK National Insurance net so that your employer deducts National Insurance contributions from your earnings and pays an employer's contribution to ensure that you build up your full entitlement to the UK basic State Pension; unless of course you had built up sufficient contributions before you went abroad, which is probably unlikely. Alternatively, you may be eligible to apply to pay voluntary Class 3 NI contributions and in some cases you may opt to pay Class 2 instead, a saving of over £5 a week! There are very complex rules regarding National Insurance contributions in these circumstances, so do take advice.

If you retire abroad, you will still be able to claim your UK State Pension, provided you have met all the necessary qualifying contributions and have of course reached State retirement age; but you will not get the yearly increases that are normally announced by the Chancellor unless you live either in the European Economic Area (EEA), or in a country that has an agreement with the UK that allows for such annual increments.

Surprisingly, in the majority of cases you can still claim the UK Winter Fuel Payment.

What is the tax situation?

If you retire abroad, you will still have to pay UK tax on any income you receive from the UK over and above your UK tax allowances; any income you receive abroad will be taxed according to local tax regulations, although as regards savings and investments you can always look at offshore banking facilities.

The Inland Revenue publish a free leaflet, *Income tax and pensioners* (IR 121), which gives useful information.

Much will depend on whether the country in which you are taking up residence has a double taxation agreement with the UK, in which case you may get taxed under local tax regulations and not that of the UK.

It is sometimes assumed that if you retire abroad you automatically become what is called non-resident for UK tax purposes. This might eventually become the goal, but the Inland Revenue will need to satisfy themselves that you are not going abroad for a trial period, or an extended holiday, before granting non-residency status. (The advantage of non-residency means that you are outside the auspices of the UK tax regime.) Your domicile will also have a bearing on your tax position. This is different from nationality or your country of residence, and is usually the place in which you have your permanent home. At birth you acquire a domicile of origin based on your father's domicile ordinarily, but this may be changed to a domicile of choice.

A detailed consideration of domicile is outside the scope of this book, and the complex rules have for some time been under review by the Government.

The disadvantages are that the rules and regulations of non-residency are fairly tough: you must not spend more than 182 days in the UK in any one tax year; and even if UK visits do not exceed 182 days, you must not spend an average of 90 days a year in the UK over a period of four tax years. Bear this in mind should you have grandchildren, relatives or an extended family in the UK!

In addition to income tax you need to know what other taxes will affect you in the country in which you live after retirement. Often the VAT rate will be higher than in the UK. You will come within the net of that country's taxation system for wealth (or inheritance) tax. In particular, in some European countries a form of death duty is payable when estates pass between husband and wife, which is not the case in the UK, and sometimes a foreign residence tax may also be applied.

Capital gains tax

If you want to sell an asset after you retire, wait until the tax year following your departure to escape this tax's clutches, and even then you have to wait five years and remain a non-resident. To generalise about capital gains tax in these circumstances is risky, for there can be different rules for different assets; so do take professional advice, particularly as the UK tax rules can change from year to year.

Inheritance tax

This is not at all simple. There are regulations stipulating how many years you have to live abroad prior to death to avoid UK inheritance tax, as well as complicated formulas as to your residence and domicile over the previous 20 years prior to death; again seek professional advice.

What other pitfalls might there be?

If you retire to an EEA country that has a reciprocal agreement with the UK on social security matters, then you should be able to claim any such benefits to which you would normally be entitled if you had stayed in the UK. Obviously some benefits will not be applicable (e.g. Housing Benefit), so you need to check this through very thoroughly. The Department for Work and Pensions publish a useful free booklet entitled *Going abroad and social security benefits* (GI 29). A further leaflet on social security benefits abroad, number SA 29, is also useful.

Finally, the DSS overseas branch (at Tyneview Park, Newcastle upon Tyne NE98 1YX) publish a leaflet on your social security health care and pension rights in the European Community, which is worth reading. Each social security benefit has its own regulations and rules so do check each one through carefully – don't automatically assume that because you are entitled to a particular benefit then that applies to all other benefits.

If you retire overseas, what about your health care? In the European Community countries you can get State health care locally on the same basis as that in the UK until you reach UK retirement age; a form E106 will need to be completed and you can get this from the Department for Work and Pensions (Overseas Contributions) – see address in Chapter 17.

Once you have reached retirement age, another form needs to be completed, namely E121, obtainable from the International Pensions Centre, and this will entitle you to free health care. As in the UK, you can always take out private health insurance as an additional security or if you want quicker attention, but the cost is not tax deductible.

Save up for health care through a commercial health plan, set aside some of your annuity or set up an ISA savings account. It's just common sense that if you are going to save for a contingency then at least get the savings working for you. Watch the 'age trap' and income levels (see Chapter 4), and remember social security benefit limits.

Older people moving to the UK

In the event that you have been living abroad and are considering coming back to live in this country then there are a multitude of factors that you will have to consider. Most of them will be outside the scope of this book and will be governed by immigration controls. You are advised to seek advice on your status, and what support or benefits you will receive, by contacting the Joint Council for the Welfare of

Immigrants at 115 Old Street, London EC1V 9RT (telephone 020 7251 8706).

You will have to check that the income you currently receive abroad will continue, and that it can be remitted to this country.

The UK State Pension is based on the number of contributions that you have paid into the fund over your lifetime; sometimes there are reciprocal arrangements with overseas countries, particularly in the European Community.

As to other social security benefits, much will depend on your intention in settling in the UK, but if your status will be someone who can be regarded as *habitually resident* (for example moving back to a house you previously occupied) then under these circumstances you may be eligible for the normal UK social security benefits.

The tax that you pay on your income will be covered by the normal UK tax rules as covered generally throughout this book; and you can check with The Pension Service to get an estimate of your State Pension entitlement (see Chapter 5).

CHAPTER 12

Giving to charity

Throughout this book there have been many times when much criticism has been directed at the UK tax system, either because it is patently unfair or inequitable – or downright immoral – or because it has been unnecessarily complicated, which has put millions of people off claiming their due rights.

However, in the case of giving to charity there has indeed been a vast improvement, in both the simplification of the tax relief structure and the accessibility for the individual, and indeed for companies.

Until 1999 the main way in which an individual could give to charity was by either leaving an asset or money in a will, or making a donation by way of a deed of covenant, thereby getting the amount allowed for tax.

In April 2000, major changes were announced by the Inland Revenue and these are covered in this chapter.

Old deeds of covenant

These covenants had to be for a minimum of three years. You deduct tax from the payment at the basic rate and can claim additional relief if you are a higher-rate taxpayer by filling in box 15A.1 in your tax return. The charity could claim back the tax for their own benefit.

Now that other schemes have been introduced, there is no need to effect this type of laborious and inflexible covenant, but if you have ongoing deeds of covenant to charities these can still continue and will be allowed for tax.

Payroll-giving schemes

If you have not yet fully retired, you may still have the option of joining an employer's payroll-giving scheme. First, your employer enters into an arrangement with one of the Inland-Revenue-approved charities agencies, such as the Charities Aid Foundation. Then the donation you wish to make is deducted from your pay and passed on to the charity selected by you. PAYE tax is calculated on your salary *after* making the donation to the charity, so you are getting immediate tax relief at your highest effective tax rate. There is no minimum or maximum amount.

Obviously your employer has to agree to the scheme but you do not need to tell your employer to which charities you are donating, as this information is between you and the charity agency.

In the event that you have other income apart from your employment, which takes you into the higher-rate tax bracket, and you have only had relief at basic rate from the deduction made by your employer, then you effectively get relief by including your salary after deducting the donation in your tax return in box 1.8; your P60 form from your employer should show this net amount.

The Government contributed a further 10 per cent to all such payroll donations for the four years to April 2004.

Gift Aid

You can make single gifts at any time to a charity and the charity gets the benefit of the tax relief, as your gift is regarded by the Inland Revenue as having been made after deducting basic relief tax. So, if you give a charity £10 then the gross equivalent of this is £12.82 and the tax thereon of £2.82 can be reclaimed by the charity. However, be warned: *You can only do this if you are a taxpayer; if you do not pay tax, not only are you unable to get the relief but also you will have to reimburse the Inland Revenue for the tax 'deducted'.*

If you are a higher-rate taxpayer, you can claim additional relief by filling in Q15A on your tax return.

How do the Inland Revenue know you have made this donation to a charity? All charities have a Gift Aid form that you must complete if they are to get the tax relief – it's a very, very simple form and basically you are confirming that you are a taxpayer and therefore the charity can reclaim the tax. This also applies to church collections, incidentally. Most churches have envelope schemes whereby your contribution effectively ranks for tax relief and you can declare it in your tax return to get higher-rate relief. You will also be asked to complete a Gift Aid confirmation if you are sponsoring someone who is engaging in an endeavour for a charity, so that the charity can reclaim tax on your sponsorship donation. So remember to keep a note of all contributions.

Again, a reminder: Do not use the Gift Aid scheme if you are not a taxpayer.

Another advantage of Gift Aid is that you can elect to backdate the gift you have made in one tax year to be reclassified as having been made in the previous tax year. Why would you want to do that? Well, suppose last year you were a higher-rate taxpayer, and this year you are a basic-rate taxpayer (perhaps, for example, you have retired); you would get more tax relief by backdating this year's Gift Aid donations into last year. You can do this by filling in box 15A.3 in your tax return. Similarly, in box 15A.4 you can treat any payments made between the end of the tax year and the date you file that return (up to 31 January in the tax year) backdated to the year covered by the tax return. It is up to you, not the Inland Revenue, to decide whether you wish to do this.

The Inland Revenue publish a useful free booklet on all aspect of this subject – it's called *Giving to charity* (IR65) and is available from all tax offices or by looking at their web site on www.hmrc.gov.uk.

Donate your tax refund

If you are due a tax refund, you can donate it directly to a charity of your choice – this has been effective from 6 April 2003 and the tax return has a special section (Q19A) to enable you to do this. You have to state the charity reference number that you want to benefit. If you don't know this number, telephone the charity helpline on 0845 302 0203.

Gifts of shares, land, buildings, etc.

Not only can you gift sums of cash as described above – the tax legislation has, over the past couple of years, made it easy for you to gift shares, security, land and buildings to charities. You can gift the full market value as well as the cost of transfer, and these can be offset against your taxable income. Additionally, such a gift (or transfer) is free of capital gains tax and inheritance tax. You should enter the amount in boxes 15A.4 and 15A.5 of your tax return. There is no limit to the value of such gifts.

Legacies

Under your will you can leave money and assets to the benefit of a charity, and such legacies are deducted from the value of your estate for inheritance tax purposes.

CHAPTER 13

Wills

It is amazing in this day and age how many people have not taken out a will. It is essential for your own peace of mind and that of your relatives and friends that you do so, particularly if you own a house.

Without wishing to cause undue alarm, let's establish straight away that in the case of a married couple, then on the death of the first partner the house – *provided it was held as joint tenants* – will automatically pass to the surviving partner even if there is no will.

To stress how important it is to make a will, take the imaginary situation of John and Mary, a married couple, where no will existed; in death, either would be deemed to have died intestate. If John died first, his estate would be distributed as follows:

- Only the first £125,000 will go to Mary, so if the house was not in joint tenancy and John's half was worth more than this figure, the house may have to be sold in order for the estate to be distributed according to intestate law.
- If there are children, then Mary will receive additionally a life interest in half of the remainder of the estate and the personal effects. The children get the rest.
- If there are no surviving children, John's parents will inherit half the balance in excess of £200,000 and Mary will get the personal effects.
- Finally, if there are no surviving children or parents, any brothers or sisters that John had will inherit half the balance in excess of £200,000 (Mary gets the personal effects); and if there are no living brothers or sisters then their children inherit.

So, you will see that poor John may have assumed that if he died before his wife she would inherit all his assets and possessions, but that would not be the case, and Mary and their family would be involved in a lot of worry and distress merely because he did not take out a will.

At this point it is worth explaining that there are two ways in which property may be held jointly. If John and Mary held their home as joint tenants, it would automatically pass to Mary on John's death. This is the normal situation for a married couple. The alternative is tenancy in common. Any assets held by John and Mary as tenants in common would form part of John's estate in respect of his share and would therefore be subject to the normal intestacy rules.

The situation can be even more traumatic for people who are unmarried or an unmarried couple (and the law does not recognise the fact that you may have been living together out of wedlock for dozens of years). This is what happens if an unmarried person (i.e. single) dies without making a will. Their estate will be distributed as follows:

- Any children inherit the entire estate, with it being shared equally between them or, if they are dead, their children.
- If there are no children, the parents will inherit the estate equally.
- If the parents are no longer alive, any brothers or sisters or their children will inherit.
- If none of the above are alive, grandparents and aunts and uncles come into the equation.
- If there are no relatives, all the assets go to the Crown (to use legal jargon).

So, to sum up – MAKE A WILL!

Same-sex couples

Same-sex couples can be treated as a couple if they have entered into a statutory civil registration procedure from December 2005, but they have to amend their wills accordingly.

How to make a will

There are do-it-yourself kits available on the market, but it is wiser to go to a solicitor who will prepare a simple will for you.

It is likely to cost around £150, although this will depend on how complicated you want your bequests to be and whether you have a lot of assets that have to be considered.

Ideally, you will need to choose two executors (in case one dies) and the will needs to be witnessed by two independent people. Bear in mind that anyone who witnesses a will cannot benefit under that will so do make sure that you select witnesses that you don't want to benefit from your will. Executors under a will are allowed to benefit from any bequest under the will.

How to find a solicitor

The various law societies have lists of solicitors who specialise in wills and probate. In England and Wales the helpline is 0870 606 6565, in Scotland 0131 226 7411 and in Northern Ireland 028 9023 1614. You can also contact the Society of Trust and Estate Practitioners, who will tell you of local solicitors who are members.

Powers of attorney

Your solicitor will probably cover this when advising you on your will. See 'Enduring power of attorney' on page 83.

Deeds of variation

Deeds of variation are covered in Chapter 15 (Inheritance tax).

Your home and inheritance tax

If a husband and wife jointly own their home, they should consider holding the property as tenants in common rather than as joint tenants if inheritance tax might be a problem. That way half can be passed on to the children on the death of one of the parents. As previously mentioned, with a joint tenancy the surviving parent will take the one half automatically, despite any intention to the contrary that may be stated in the will – see also Chapter 10, Chapter 15 covers inheritance tax.

Trusts

If you are not sure what to do with your estate, you can set up a discretionary trust in the will and appoint trustees; they will have two years in which to give away your assets. You will doubtless have discussed your general intentions with your selected trustees during your lifetime, so that they have a good idea of your wishes.

Bequests to charities

Many people make reference to specific charities in their will, stating to whom they would like to make legacies. The only problem with this is that, if you wish to change the charities you have selected, you have to make a new will.

You can get over this by leaving the legacies to the Charities Aid Foundation, giving them a list of the charities you wish to benefit. You can then change this list at any time, thus saving you the legal costs of changing your will.

Capital gains tax

Previous chapters in this book have dealt mainly with income and income tax. However, another tax is lurking in the shadows – capital gains tax.

Capital gains tax sets out to tax any profit you make when you sell, transfer, receive compensation for, give away or otherwise dispose of any assets, for example land and buildings, shares, antiques, paintings or a business.

There are exemptions and allowances which are dealt with a little later on in this chapter so don't start to panic and think that everything you own is going to be taxed when you sell it. However, nowadays you could be forgiven for thinking this was the case – with the ever-increasing burden of taxation that we all have to cope with and, perhaps more to the point, the ever-increasing complexity of form filling and record keeping to which we are all endlessly subjected.

Incidentally, there is no capital gains payable on death; instead, inheritance tax comes into play (see Chapter 15).

Bear in mind that this capital gains chapter deals specifically with disposals by individuals. There are special rules for business assets and interests in trusts, which can be complicated and are outside the scope of this book.

Is there such a thing as a capital loss? Yes, obviously it is the reverse of a capital gain and any such losses can be deducted from any gain in the same tax year (6 April to 5 April). You cannot, however, claim tax back on a capital loss, but you can carry it forward to future years and offset it against any future capital gains.

Assets that are exempted from capital gains

The most important asset for most people will be *your own house*. If it is owned and occupied by you and is your main residence, this is *free of capital gains tax* – but see page 96 if it is part-let or used for business. Thus a husband and wife can have only one main residence between them; a couple who co-habit can have one residence each and are thus technically in a more favourable position tax-wise! Same-sex couples can be treated as a couple if they have entered into a statutory civil registration procedure from December 2005.

Perhaps the second most important exemption is transfers of assets between married couples. These are treated as taking place for no capital profit or loss; this does not apply if the parties are separated or divorced.

Other main assets which are exempt from this tax are:

- Personal belongings (chattels as the legislation calls them) such as jewellery, pictures and furniture, where the proceeds are £6,000 or less (this limit has remained at this level since 1970!)
- Compensation for damages
- Decorations for gallantry, unless purchased
- Foreign currency for personal use
- Gambling, pools and lottery winnings and prizes
- Gifts of outstanding public interest given to the nation
- Gifts to charities and community amateur sports clubs
- Government stocks and public corporation stocks
- A house owned and occupied by you which is your main residence; if part-let, or used for business, see below
- Individual savings accounts (ISAs), including the transfer of shares from an employee share scheme and TESSA accounts
- Interests in trusts or settlements
- Life policies and deferred annuities (unless sold on by original owner)
- National Savings and Investments
- Premium Bonds
- Personal equity plan (PEP) investments
- Private cars
- Qualifying corporate bonds
- Qualifying shares subscribed for under Venture Capital Trusts (VCTs) or the Enterprise Investment Scheme (EIS) – subject to minimum periods of ownership
- Save As You Earn schemes
- Wasting assets with a likely life of 50 years or more (e.g. antique clocks, vintage cars, a boat).

Your house: selling, letting or business use

Any profit you make on selling your main residence that you own and live in is free from capital gains tax. Where you own two houses at the same time as a result of not being able to sell the first, no capital gains will arise on either house, provided you sell the first house within three years.

In the case of a divorced or separated couple, if one partner sells, or gives the house to the other partner within three years of the separation, there will be no capital gains tax payable; and by concession there will still be no tax to pay after that period if one of the partners still resides there and the other partner has not claimed any other property as a main home, and the property is eventually transferred as part of a financial settlement.

Many people worry that if they let part of their home, then they will have to pay capital gains tax on part of the profits they make when it is sold. In fact, you can claim letting relief to reduce any capital gains liability.

You do this by working out what proportion the let part of the property bears to the total and apply this to any capital profit. Against that profit you can claim capital gains tax letting relief of £40,000 or the apportioned gain before any capital gains tax liability is assessed, whichever is the lower.

The last three years of ownership of your home always counts as a period of residence, so if you move out and let the property during that time it will not affect your exemption.

If you use part of your house exclusively for business then, when you sell the house, you may be liable to capital gains tax on that proportion that was used for business purposes, but of course you can offset your annual exemption amount (see below). You are unlikely to be regarded as using the house for business if you are an employee working from home occasionally, unless a material part of the house is in fact used exclusively for business.

Annual exemption

You are allowed to make capital gains of £8,500 a year (this is the figure for the tax year 2005–2006; it is normally increased slightly in each year's Budget in spring). This figure is after setting-off against your capital gains any capital losses that you have incurred in the year. Married couples each get this annual exemption amount but they cannot offset each other's losses against profits.

In addition to the annual exemption amount, you can claim relief for inflation, depending on how long you have held the asset (see page 98).

Can you avoid capital gains tax?

First, you should ensure that you are making full use of assets that are tax free (see Chapter 9), for example by putting some of your savings into investments like ISAs, pension schemes, National Savings, Government stocks or various Venture and Enterprise schemes.

The next thing to bear in mind is the annual exemption amount: for example, if you own shares and you have made a profit on a certain share which you are planning to sell, then it may be beneficial to sell it just before the end of the tax year (5 April) if you have not made any other capital profits that year, in order to make use of the annual exemption amount. Conversely, if you are planning on selling something at a loss, and you have made other capital profits in the year, then sell it before the tax-year end so that the loss can be offset against those capital profits that you have made in the year.

From time to time you will read in the press about capital gains avoidance schemes which some observant accountant or lawyer has come up with – usually as a result of exposing some badly worded legislation in a Finance Act. Many of these are bona fide, although in each year's Budget the Chancellor of the day usually tries to amend legislation to plug such a loophole and advisers are now required to notify the Inland Revenue of new 'schemes'. If you are tempted along this path, do make sure that you seek professional advice and be sure that you are aware of the risks as well as the advantages.

If you have gifted some of your assets, you can avoid paying capital gains tax by claiming what is known as hold-over relief. This effectively means that the person to whom you are giving gifts takes on the asset at the original cost that would have been applied if you had sold the asset yourself, and therefore also takes over any potential capital gains tax liability. Obviously you need the recipient's agreement to do this. Hold-over relief is only available to business assets, gifts to political parties and heritage property, and gifts to certain trusts, but this is more complex as they are allied to inheritance tax liabilities.

What is the capital gains tax rate?

This varies from person to person, for your capital gains tax rate is the same as your rate for income tax purposes as if it were taxed as savings income. Any capital gain that you make is added to your total income for tax purposes and this total amount will define whether your tax rate is the starting rate of 10 per cent, the savings rate of 20 per cent, or the higher rate at 40 per cent. So if you have low income and a very large gain you may pay capital gains tax at 10 per cent, 20 per cent and 40 per cent as your gain, when added to your income, exceeds each of the rate bands in turn. You cannot, however, use your income tax personal allowance to reduce any capital gain.

What is the cost of an asset for tax purposes?

First, you have to know the actual cost of the asset and the original date on which you acquired it, because there are two critical dates: assets held on or before 31 March 1982 have a different valuation basis; and those acquired after 6 April 1988 have a different inflation allowance calculation.

For assets held before 31 March 1982 you can use either their original cost (or market value if not purchased) plus expenses, or the value as at 31 March 1982, whichever gives the smaller gain or loss in each case. Alternatively, you can elect to adopt the 31 March value for all of your assets. Such an election, once made and notified to the tax inspector, cannot be changed, and the time limit for making the election is two years after the end of the tax year in which you first made a disposal after 5 April 1988.

For assets purchased or acquired since 31 March 1982, the initial purchase price (or market value if not purchased), plus acquisition expenses incurred before indexation is applied, will be the cost figure for calculating any capital gain or loss. There are additional, complicated rules for assets held on 6 April 1965 and the rules vary depending on the type of asset, so you are recommended to seek professional advice.

Some examples

- You purchased shares costing, say, £750, and sold them for £2,000. You have made a gain of £1,250, before allowing for inflation.
- On his death, your brother bequeathed some shares to you valued at £6,000. No capital gains tax is payable at that time, but if you later sell them for, say, £10,000, you will have made a gain of £4,000 before allowing for inflation.
- You purchased a flat for your daughter to use, costing £75,000. Some years later you decide to give the flat to your daughter. Its market value at that time is £100,000 so, even though your daughter may not have paid you anything for it, you have made a gain of £25,000 before allowing for inflation.

How to claim for inflation

In respect of assets held at 5 April 1998 an indexation allowance can be claimed for the period of ownership up to 30 April 1998. Thereafter, tapering relief will be applied to those assets and to assets purchased after 5 April 1998.

Indexation allowance

The indexation is based on the value at 31 March 1982 or acquisition value if acquired later, so you will need to know the value at 31 March 1982 for assets acquired before then. Refer to your tax office to obtain the percentage by which the retail prices index has increased either from 31 March 1982 or from the date you acquired the asset (if later) to April 1998, or go to their web site, www.hmrc.gov.uk.

Note that indexation can only be offset against any capital gain; it cannot be used to create or increase a capital loss.

Tapering relief

A tapering scale replaced the indexation allowance from 6 April 1998 (see table on page 101). Assets acquired before 17 March 1998 qualified for an addition of one year when applying the taper (except for business assets disposed of on or after 6 April 2000).

The taper is applied to the net gains that are chargeable after the deduction of any current year's losses and losses brought forward from earlier years. The annual exemption amount (see page 96) will then be deducted from the tapered gains.

Note that there are different figures for business assets – only individuals are covered in this book.

Purchases and sales within a 30-day period are matched so that no gain or loss will be realised for tax purposes.

What to enter in your tax return

There is a supplementary tax return on which you will need to declare any capital gains or losses. It is called SA 108. Telephone 0845 9000 404 if you have your main tax return but need this supplementary form (or ring your local tax office if you need the main tax return). The capital gains tax return can be downloaded from the web on www.hmrc.gov.uk/sa.

Capital gains in the year ended 5 April 2005 will need to be declared in your 2005 tax return. If your chargeable gains do not exceed the annual exemption level of £8,500 (for 2004–2005 this was £8,200) and/or the total proceeds of sale do not exceed four times these figures (i.e. £32,800 for 2004-2005), there is no need to make any entry in the capital gain part of your tax return.

It is important to tell the Inland Revenue if you have made a capital loss, as otherwise you may not be able to carry it forward to offset against future gains.

Do, however, keep all records and schedules, for you never know when the Inland Revenue are going to query any of your financial

---

Example of the combination of indexation allowance and tapering relief

Alfred held shares costing £10,000 in 1989 and sold them for £20,000, after deducting allowable selling costs, in March 2005.

	£	£
Disposal proceeds		20,000
Cost	10,000	
Indexation allowance from 1989 to 1998 based on Inland Revenue index, say	4,000	14,000
Gain before taper relief		£ 6,000

Tapering relief*: seven years' taper relief (see chart) means that the gain of £6,000 is reduced to 75% × £6,000, giving Alfred a chargeable gain of £4,500. (*Six years plus one extra year, as the asset was held prior to 17 March 1998.)

This is less than the annual exemption amount of £8,200 for 2004–2005, so Alfred will not have a capital gains tax liability if this was his only sale in the year.

Notes
1. If the shares had been held prior to 31 March 1982, the value at that date would have been used as the cost if it was higher than the original cost.
2. If you elect to re-base the cost of an asset to its 1982 value, all chargeable assets have to be valued that way; you cannot be selective.

---

affairs. Individuals need to keep records for 22 months from the end of the tax year or five years and ten months if self-employed.

When do you have to pay the tax?

Capital gains tax is payable, together with any balance of income tax due, on the following 31 January after each tax year. Here is a useful tax tip: if you sell an asset on which you have a capital gain on 6 April rather than 5 April, you will effectively have an extra year before you have to pay the capital gains tax.

The only way you can defer paying any capital gains tax if you are an individual, as distinct from a business, is to consider investing

Capital gains tapering relief chart
(non-business assets)

Number of complete years after 5 April 1998 for which asset held	Percentage of gain chargeable
0	100
1	100
2	100
3	95
4	90
5	85
6	80
7	75
8	70
9	65
10 or more	60

Note: One extra year is added if the asset was owned on or before 17 March 1998.

in an Enterprise Investment Scheme (EIS) or purchase shares in an approved Venture Capital Trust (VCT) (see page 73).

Inherited assets

Contrary to many people's belief you do not generally have to pay capital gains tax on receiving cash or assets left to you under a will or settlement. Assets only become liable (subject to the normal exemption rules) when you dispose of them.

Windfalls from building societies, etc.

It has been common practice over the last few years for mutual insurance companies to pay out 'windfall proceeds' to their members.

These are liable to capital gains tax if, when added to any other capital gains you have incurred, the total exceeds the annual exemption amount (see page 96). This area has become more complex of late with some schemes being designed by insurance companies to avoid their members paying capital gains tax, so do read any paperwork carefully, and contact the insurance company or your tax office if you are unclear.

Seek professional advice

If your financial affairs are not too complicated, capital gains tax can be fairly straightforward. However, only a brief outline of the tax has been covered in this book, so do seek professional advice if you are in any way unclear about the taxable effects of selling or gifting assets.

For more background information the Inland Revenue issue a free leaflet, CGT/FS1, available from any tax office.

CHAPTER 15

Inheritance tax

Throughout your life you will probably have been taxed at almost every stage. When you started work and received a salary it was taxed (income tax); in addition to which you also paid National Insurance contributions, which is a tax by another name; when you invested that hard-earned salary, tax was probably deducted from the net sum received and if you made a profit you were taxed (capital gains tax); when you purchased petrol for your car you were taxed (fuel duty) and similarly with most other purchases (VAT).

Having spent your life paying tax, you would have thought that it was only equitable that what you had acquired in terms of assets – your house, savings, chattels, etc. – were safe from tax and could have been passed on to your family (or whoever) without having to pay yet more tax to the Chancellor of the day!

Sadly, that is not of course the case, for inheritance tax will be looming over you or, to be precise, your wife, husband, partner or heirs.

It was not many years ago when a vast majority of people assumed, quite correctly, that inheritance tax was only paid by the really well off. But with the appreciation of assets – particularly the family home over the past ten years, and perhaps property or assets from grandparents having passed to their children – more and more people are receiving an unpleasant surprise in realising that their estate could be liable for inheritance tax.

The exemption limit for inheritance tax for 2005–2006 is only £275,000, rising to £300,000 by 2007–2008; and when you consider the current value of your house, any savings and investments you may have – perhaps also proceeds from life assurance, pension fund lump sums and various chattels (e.g. pictures, cars, collections of stamps, etc.) – then you can see that your estate could easily exceed the exempted amount.

Perhaps the opening paragraphs in this chapter are a little alarmist, but this is deliberate in order to raise the alert, so let's look more specifically into this tax and go through it step by step.

What are your total assets (less liabilities)?

In other words, what is the current value (and thus the likely future value when you die) of your estate?

You will need to make a list of all your assets and add up their value to see how close you are likely to be to the inheritance tax exemption limit (see page 103). When you have identified this total, you can deduct from it the following:

- Any mortgages, loans and creditors outstanding
- Legacies made for the benefit of the nation or for the public benefit, including funds to maintain historic property
- Legacies made between husband and wife, provided both are domiciled in the UK
- Legacies to a charity
- Legacies to political parties
- Legacies of certain heritage property and woodlands.

Now it gets a little more complicated. Having established your net worth (assets, less liabilities and legacies), you have to add on to this total any gifts that you have made during the previous seven years; but the definition of gifts is rather involved.

Gifts fall into three categories as far as the inheritance tax rules are concerned: some gifts are specifically exempt; other gifts are exempt provided they were not made within seven years of death; and the third category covers any other gifts.

Gifts

(a) Specifically exempt gifts

The following gifts are exempt:

1. All gifts between a husband and wife, provided both are domiciled in the UK (if not, a £55,000 limit applies).
2. Gifts up to a total of £3,000 in any one year, plus any unused amount of the previous year's exemption. (You can carry over unused relief for a maximum of one year.)
3. In addition to the £3,000 referred to above, individual gifts not exceeding £250 each to different persons in any one tax year (to an unlimited number of people as long as they don't form part of a larger gift).
4. Additional gifts if a person makes them as part of normal expenditure made out of income.

5. Gifts arranged beforehand in consideration of marriage – as follows:

Inheritance tax exemption on wedding gifts	
Giver	Gift limit £
Bridegroom to bride or vice versa	2,500
Parents of either	5,000 each
Grandparents or more remote relatives of either	2,500
Any other person	1,000
(The gifts must be made before the actual wedding day.)	

6. All gifts to political parties, or UK-established charities.
7. Lump sums received from a pension scheme on death or retirement if used to purchase a pension for yourself or dependants.
8. Gifts for the benefit of the nation or public (e.g. universities, the National Trust).
9. Maintenance payments to ex-husbands or ex-wives.
10. Reasonable gifts to support a dependent relative.
11. Gifts for the education and maintenance of your children, if under 18.

(b) Gifts under the seven-year rule
In tax jargon these are called potentially exempt gifts. They include gifts to individuals rather than those in the exempt list (above); gifts into accumulation, and maintenance trusts and gifts into trust for the disabled, provided the donor lives for at least seven years from the date of the gift. If the person making the gift dies within a shorter time, there is tapering relief as follows:

Years between gift and death	0–3	3–4	4–5	5–6	6–7
Percentage of inheritance tax payable:	100	80	60	40	20

(c) Other gifts
Other gifts would normally cover transfers to a discretionary trust and the like, and any tax is normally payable at the time the gift is made, once the total value of such gifts made within the seven-year rule goes above the total exemption limit (usually the tax is paid by the person receiving the gift, although it can be paid by the donor).

Calculating the tax payable

There are only two inheritance tax rates – nil and 40 per cent; there is no correlation between the inheritance tax rate and your personal income tax rate.

If the value of your estate as compiled above is below £275,000 for 2005–2006, then the rate is nil. If it is over £275,000, the rate is 40 per cent on any excess over that figure.

There are three glimmers of light that can reduce the tax payable:

1. under the seven-year gift rules already mentioned above there is tapering relief depending on the length of time between making the gift and the date of death as detailed above.
2. there is relief if a second death in a family occurs within one year of the first death. This is called quick succession relief and the second tax bill is reduced by the ratio that the value of the estate on the first death bears to the value at the second death, to which needs to be added any inheritance tax paid on that first death. For example, assume the value of the estate at the first death was £400,000, on which inheritance tax was paid, and the estate value at the second death was £500,000, then the inheritance tax bill on the estate of the second death would be reduced by the ratio 5:4.
3. under quick succession relief, above, if there were more than one year between the two deaths, the calculation is reduced by 20 per cent for each complete year.

Who pays the inheritance tax bill?

It is the responsibility of the executors of a will to pay any taxes due before distributing the assets to the beneficiaries. However, in the case of gifts made within the seven-year rule, executors could ask the person receiving the gift to pay the tax relating to the value of that gift, unless there is a clause in the will specifically authorising the estate to be responsible for paying any tax due.

It is important both to remember that the inheritance tax has to be paid before assets can be distributed, and to emphasise the fact that all the assets are therefore frozen until the tax liability is agreed and settled.

Can you reduce or eliminate inheritance tax?

Many years ago, when far fewer estates came into the inheritance tax bracket, it was said that this tax was a voluntary tax because, as it mainly concerned wealthier estates, such people had the financial means to employ good accountants and lawyers to so arrange their affairs that no tax would ever have to be paid if such professionals did their job properly. However, with more and more people falling into the inheritance tax net it is important to be aware of some of the ways that you can reduce or avoid this tax without getting involved in really elaborate and complicated tax planning and structures.

The following ideas are worth considering and are biased towards the assumption that your home is your main asset, the value of which is taking you into an inheritance tax liability situation; it is therefore that particular asset that you need to protect or take out of the total asset equation.

Nine ways to combat inheritance tax

1. Make sure you have made a will. See the detailed coverage about the wisdom of making a will – and what happens if you don't – in Chapter 13.
2. Put your main assets (e.g. your house, investments) into joint names if you are married – this, at a stroke will reduce the value of total assets in the event of the first partner dying. On that death, because the asset is jointly owned, it will automatically pass to the husband or wife unless the will states otherwise. This, however, might be only a short-term solution because on the death of the second partner that estate will be subject to inheritance tax if no ongoing plan of mitigation is adopted. Thought should therefore be given to the following ideas.
3. In the case of a home a married couple could consider taking out a life assurance policy putting it into trust, say, for their children; the policy pays out on the second death (the property having passed to the husband or wife on the first death and not incurring inheritance tax). On the second death, the house value is not taken into the estate as it will have been written in trust for the children. The policy premiums paid could be considered to be gifts to the children (see above), or indeed the children could pay the premiums if they could afford them. If you can't afford to take out a policy, perhaps take out a small mortgage to provide the funds to pay for a single life assurance premium (to effect an insurance as above). The pay-out would be free of inheritance tax but you would of course have been paying out mortgage interest.
4. If the above options are not appropriate, you may need to consider equity release schemes (see Chapter 10).
5. *Tenancies in common:* If a married couple own their house in joint names, that is normally considered a joint tenancy – in the event of a change (e.g. wanting to sell) then each party must agree. In the UK (excluding Scotland) there is an alternative called

'tenancies in common' under which each party's share (and it does not have to be in equal parts) is independent of the other and can be sold or given away as that party wishes. To reduce any inheritance tax liability, such share in the property could be left to children or grandchildren, etc. If you share a property and you are not married but living with a partner, on the death of one of the partners their share, if passing to the surviving partner, could be liable to inheritance tax if their share was above the exemption limit (£275,000 for 2005–2006). Contact a solicitor if you are living together as partners to plan for avoiding this situation. Also note that same-sex partners who register their relationship in a civil partnership after 21 December 2005 will be entitled to the same tax benefits as married couples.

6. *Discretionary and other trusts:* Much is written in the media about effecting various types of trust to mitigate inheritance tax. Yes, some of these can work, but it is essential that they are talked through with a solicitor, and do remember that once you have parted with an asset, particularly your home, by setting up a trust you have given up control of that asset and cannot have any influence on what happens to it in the future. There needs to be a great deal of understanding and trust between the parties concerned if, say, your house is to be placed into trust. You cannot simply pass it on to a trust and assume that you can live in it, unless you pay a commercial rate of rent. As mentioned earlier, legislation has been effected of late to tighten up drastically on the use of trusts to limit or avoid inheritance tax liabilities. Discretionary and Discounted Gift Trusts which are currently marketed by insurance companies circumvent the legislation at present, but do seek professional advice.

7. Make sure that you utilise the 'nil rate' band. It is all very well a husband, say, leaving his estate to his wife (which on his death would not incur inheritance tax), but this really just delays a potential inheritance tax liability on his wife's death. It would be better for the wife to bequeath an amount within the nil-rate band (under £275,000 in 2005–2006) to their children (or whoever) so that this will effectively reduce the value of the estate that eventually passes on the death of the wife.

8. *Deed of Variation:* If the will did not make provision for using the nil rate band by a bequest or whatever (as above), then a Deed of Variation can be effected following the first death so that the nil-rate value can miss passing to the wife and pass instead to an appointed beneficiary, or via a discretionary trust (see above). The

deed must be effected within two years of the date of death.
9. Consider investments in woodlands, agricultural property or shares quoted on the Alternative Investment Market (AIM) and Enterprise Investment Schemes, because these are exempt from inheritance tax, provided they are held for two years.

Always remember that it is not just a question of passing an asset over to your children or someone else on the assumption that such legal transfer will avoid inheritance tax. You must also give up 'using' it yourself. For example, suppose you owned a holiday home, gifted it to your children but then carried on using it yourself and paying the bills, then that would not be deemed a gift without reservation, which it needs to be to escape the tax liability. Your children would need to pay all bills and be seen to be maintaining it – you can still have a holiday there, but as a guest!

Special rules for businesses and certain other assets

There are special valuation rules and reduced rates of tax for business property, shares in an unlisted company and agricultural property, certain gifts to preservation trusts, historic houses and works of art.

In the case of small businesses and agricultural concerns there have been many concessions announced in the annual Budgets over the last few years, and it is very important that you seek professional guidance in the event that you have a holding in such businesses, and ensure that whoever is handling your estate probate is well qualified in the current legislation, or at least has access to such advice.

Inheritance tax avoidance (pre-owned assets)

As from Budget Day, 16 March 2005, the Inland Revenue cracked down on certain schemes and trusts used by thousands of elderly people to keep their homes outside their estate for inheritance tax purposes, particularly those arrangements where people have given away assets while still retaining a benefit from them.

For example, double trusts, as some of these home loan schemes were called, involved your selling your house to a trust in return for an IOU payable on your death (known as Eversden trusts); another such trust, the Ingram trust scheme, included giving part of your home to your partner in a life interest trust, subsequently being terminated in favour of your children.

If you have been involved in setting up such schemes to avoid inheritance tax, you will need to get professional advice to see if you will be affected, for the legislation is complicated.

If you do fall foul of the legislation, you will have three main options:

(a) you can pay an income tax charge as a 'benefit'

(b) you can unravel the trust

(c) you can tell the Inland Revenue to assume that you never made the gift and thus the asset remains part of the estate for inheritance tax.

Options (b) and (c) are available until 31 January 2007.

CHAPTER 16

Frequently asked questions

*Page
reference*

**Should I worry about the new pension legislation
starting in April 2006?**
Yes, you should get your pension scheme(s) reviewed before
this date to make sure that any tax-advantageous amounts are
pre-registered; it also gives you the opportunity to see if you
should invest more in the scheme before April 2006.   47

**Is my pension protected if the pension provider
or my employer goes under?**
Not necessarily, it depends on the type of scheme.   43

How will my divorce affect any pension entitlement?
This will depend on the details of the divorce settlement
and the negotiations between all parties and your solicitor.   47

**I worked for a company 25 years ago and paid into
a pension scheme. How can I check if I have any
pension rights?**
Contact the Pension Schemes Registry for them to do a
search for you.   45

**I have had a windfall allowance from a building society
following a merger. Is it taxable?**
You need to check with the building society or the Inland
Revenue. Capital gains tax might be payable, but every
scheme has to be considered individually.   69

**I am not claiming the Winter Fuel Payment because
it's means-tested. Is that right?**
No. It is not means-tested. Most households with somone
aged over 60 are entitled to it.   114

**Where can I put my savings so I do not have to worry
about tax?**
There are many savings schemes that do not deduct tax
from the income – and you do not have to declare the
details in your tax return.   67

**Can I give money to my grandchildren without them
having to pay tax?**
Yes, there are several useful ideas listed in this book.   75

CHAPTER 17

Useful contacts

Taxation matters

To download tax forms: www.hmrc.gov.uk/sa

Requests for supplementary tax return sheets: 0845 9000 404

To file your tax return electronically: www.online.inland
revenue.gov.uk

Inland Revenue general tax advice helpline: 0845 9000 444

Claiming tax back that has been deducted from interest:
0845 077 6543

Pension Credit claim line: 0800 99 1234; 0808 100 6165 (Northern
Ireland)

Child Tax Credit helpline: 0845 300 3900; 0845 603 2000 (Northern
Ireland); claim line 0800 500 2220

Tax credit information generally: www.taxcredits.inlandrevenue.gov.uk

Child Trust Fund helpline: 0845 302 1471;
www.childtrustfund.gov.uk

To get copies of various free booklets published by the Inland
Revenue: www.hmrc.gov.uk/leaflets/index.htm

Social security matters

Winter Fuel Payment queries: 0845 915 1515

Department for Work and Pensions: 0845 606 0265;
www.dwp.gov.uk

Pension matters

The Pensions Advisory Service (OPAS): 0845 601 2923;
www.opas.org.uk

International Pension Centre: 0191 218 7777;
www.thepensionservice.gov.uk/contact

The Pensions Regulator (took over from the Occupational Pensions
Regulatory Authority (OPRA) on 6 April 2005): 0191 225 6316;
www.thepensionsregulator.gov.uk

Government Pensions Helpline: 0845 731 3233

State Pension Forecasting Service: 0845 300 0168;
www.thepensionservice.gov.uk

The Pensions Ombudsman: 020 7834 9144;
www.pensions-ombudsman.org.uk

State Pension Enquiry Service: 0845 300 1084

The Pension Service: www.thepensionservice.gov.uk

State Pension deferral booklet: 08457 313 233

Other useful web sites: www.over50.gov.uk;
www.agepositive.gov.uk and www.jobcentreplus.gov.uk

Annuity quotes: www.betterannuities.co.uk

Savings and investment matters

National Savings and Investments: 0845 964 5000; www.nsandi.com

Government stocks registrar: 0800 818 614

Association of Investment Trust Companies: 020 7282 5555;
www.aitc.co.uk or www.trustnet.co.uk

Safe Home Income plans: www.ship-ltd.org

Financial Ombudsman Service (FOS): 0845 080 1800;
www.financial-ombudsman.org.uk

Financial Services Authority (FSA): 0845 606 1234;
www.fsa.gov.uk/consumer

Financial Services Compensation Scheme (FSCS): 020 7892 7300;
www.fscs.org.uk

ISA helpline regarding tax queries: 0845 604 1701

Miscellaneous

Help the Aged Seniorline: 0808 800 6565; www.helptheaged.org.uk

Age Concern information line: 0800 00 9966;
www.ageconcern.org.uk

Charities Aid Foundation: 01732 520000

Just Retirement: www.justretirement.net

National Insurance Contributions Office (NICO): 0191 213 5000;
www.hmrc.gov.uk

Law Society helplines regarding solicitors who specialise in wills
and probate:
England and Wales: 0870 606 6565
Scotland: 0831 226 7411
Northern Ireland: 028 9023 1614

How to define your total income

Income that is taxable

All of the following types of income must be added together in order to define your total income for tax purposes.

- Annuities that you have received (include the gross amount before any tax has been deducted)
- Benefits from an employer (e.g. company car, health benefits); the figure to include is the one stated on the P11D form, which your employer will have sent to the Inland Revenue and of which they have, by law, to give you a copy
- Bereavement Allowance
- Carer's Allowance
- Casual income you have earned either from occasional work or from a hobby, etc., but remember to include only the net amount after you have deducted all relevant expenses
- Compensation for mis-selling (other than pensions), although there is a court case challenging whether this is taxable on any amount in excess of the return of the premium paid
- Dividends from shares – include the gross amount before taking off the tax credit; also dividends from Accumulation Unit Trusts (even if they are added to your capital and you don't actually receive them)
- Incapacity Benefit (except the first 28 weeks)
- Incentive schemes
- Income from building societies and banks – include the amounts before deducting any tax (send in your book regularly to have it updated for interest,etc.)
- Income from unit trusts
- Income withdrawals from a delayed annuity pension plan
- Industrial Death Benefit
- Jobseeker's Allowance – up to capped amounts
- Luncheon vouchers – any excess over 15p a day. Yes, really!
- National Savings bank interest from all accounts (excluding the first £70 of interest from an ordinary account)

- National Savings Bond income
- Pension income – show the gross amount before any tax that may have been deducted
- Purchased life annuity – the income proportion
- Rent and key monies (but not Rent-a-Room income) after expenses
- Reverse premiums
- Royalties
- State Pension including any supplementary graduated pension and SERPS, etc.
- Statutory sick pay; maternity, adoption and paternity pay
- Stipends received by the clergy
- Stock and scrip dividends
- Trust income (gross)
- Unit trust income before any tax is deducted
- Wages, salaries and bonuses (gross – before any deductions), including any holiday pay or payments in lieu
- Widowed Parent's Allowance (or Widowed Mother's Allowance)
- Widow's Pension.

Income that is not taxable

You do not have to include any of the following income or benefits in your total income calculations, nor in your tax return.

- Adoption allowances and most foster care payments
- Annuities for gallantry awards
- Attendance Allowance
- Awards for damages
- Benefits from certain insurance policies if you are sick, disabled or unemployed at the time the benefit becomes payable
- Bereavement payments
- Car parking benefits
- Child Benefit and allowances
- Child dependency additions paid by the State
- Child Tax Credit
- Christmas Bonus paid by the State to pensioners
- Cold weather payments
- Compensation for loss of office (up to £30,000)
- Compensation monies received for mis-sold personal pensions (in the case of mis-sold AVCs, lump sums can be excluded but if you receive annual payments they must be included)
- Council Tax Benefit
- Council tax contribution paid to pensioners
- Disabled Person's Tax Credit

- Disablement Pensions from the Armed Forces
- Disability and Wounds Pensions
- Disability Living Allowance
- Education grants and awards from a local authority or school
- Employment grants from Government schemes
- Endowment policy receipts
- Family Income Supplement and Family Credit
- Foreign Service Allowance paid to servants of the Crown
- Foster Carer's Income (although this is a complicated area – telephone the helpline 020 7438 6420, to check your situation)
- Gifts
- Grants from local authorities, etc. for insulation and home repairs
- Gratuities from the Armed Forces
- Guardian's Allowance
- Home improvement grants
- Housing Benefit
- Incapacity Benefit (if claiming Invalidity Benefit since 12 April 1995)
- Industrial Injury Benefit
- Income from ISAs, TESSAs, PEPs, TOISAs
- Income Support – unless you are also getting Jobseeker's Allowance, in which case it goes in the 'Income that is taxable' list
- Industrial Injuries Disablement Pension
- Interest from the Inland Revenue
- Invalidity Pension
- Investment bond withdrawals up to 5 per cent a year (but check with your insurance company as there are numerous types of policy)
- Jobseeker's Allowance above the taxable maximum
- Long-service awards up to £50 for each year of service (gifts but not cash)
- Lump sums from pension schemes (unless they did not have Inland Revenue approval – there may also be a cap on the amount that is free of tax)
- Maintenance or alimony
- Maternity Allowance
- Miners' Coal Allowance
- Minimum Income Guarantee
- National Savings Certificate income
- National Savings ordinary account interest (the first £70 of interest)
- One Parent Benefit
- Overseas pension (the first 10 per cent)
- Pension Credit

- Pensions as a result of Nazi persecution
- Personal injury compensation
- Prizes and winnings (e.g. from Premium Bonds, Lotto, football pools and betting winnings)
- Provident benefits up to £4,000 lump sum benefits
- Purchased life annuities – the capital portion of yearly amounts
- Redundancy payments (up to £30,000)
- Rent-a-Room rental income up to prescribed limit
- Rent rebates
- SAYE bonuses
- Share option profits
- Sickness benefits under an insurance policy for up to 12 months, where the premiums are paid by the employee
- Social Fund payments
- Strike and unemployment pay from a trade union
- Subsidised free bus travel to work
- Training allowances
- Venture Capital Trust dividends
- War Disablement Pensions
- War Widow's Benefits
- War Widow's Pensions
- Windfalls from some building societies, etc. following a merger – check with the society for each one is considered on its own merit (see page 69)
- Winter Fuel Payment
- Working Tax Credit and Working Families' Tax Credit.

Child Tax Credit and Working Tax Credit

There are numerous elements making up the Child Tax Credit, most of which are governed by the amount of your total earnings.

The following chart, based on figures for 2005–2006, is issued by the Inland Revenue as a *general guide* to see at a glance whether you could be eligible to claim.

Child Tax Credit

Gross annual income	One child annual	Two children annual	Three children annual
£	£	£	£
5,000 or under	2,240	3,930	5,625
10,000	3,930	2,240	5,625
15,000	1,835	3,530	5,525
20,000	545	1,680	3,375
25,000–50,000	545	545	1,525
55,000	210	210	210
60,000	0	0	0

You receive a higher rate of Child Tax Credit in the first year of a new baby's life, it is paid in the year following the baby's birth.

Working Tax Credit (WTC)

There are numerous elements making up the Working Tax Credit.

The following charts, based on figures for 2005–2006, are issued by the Inland Revenue as a *general guide* so that you can see at a glance whether you could be eligible to claim.

You will receive a higher rate of Working Tax Credit if: you are aged 50 or more and have just returned to work after qualifying for out-of-work benefits; or you are a working person disadvantaged from getting a job because of a disability; or you have a severe disability.

Child Tax Credit[3] and Working Tax Credit
If you are responsible for at least one child or young person

Gross annual joint income £	One child £	Two children £
5,000[1]	5,455	7,150
8,000[2]	5,085	6,780
10,000	4,345	6,040
15,000	2,495	4,190
20,000	645	2,340
25,000–50,000	545	545
55,000	210	210
60,000	0	0

Notes
1. Those with income of £5,000 a year are assumed to work part-time (working between 16 and 30 hours a week).
2. In families with an income of £8,000 a year or more, at least one adult is assumed to be working 30 hours or more a week.
3. If you have a child under one year old, you may be entitled to more Child Tax Credit.
4. If you are eligible for WTC you may get a contribution towards a registered or approved childminder to look after your child.

Working Tax Credit
If you are not responsible for any children or young people

Gross annual income £	Single person aged 25 or over working 30 or more hours a week £	Couple (working adult aged 25 or over) working 30 or more hours a week £
7,566[1]	1,410	3,005
8,000	1,250	2,845
10,000	510	2,105
12,000	0	1,365
14,000	0	625

Note
1. Someone aged 25 or over, working 30 hours a week on National Minimum Wage, would earn £7,566 a year.

Rates of tax and allowances

	2005–2006	2004–2005	2003–2004
Income tax			
Starting rate at 10 per cent	£2,090	£2,020	£1,960
Basic rate at 22 per cent	£2,091–£32,400	£2,021–£31,400	£1,960–£30,500
Higher rate at 40 per cent	over £32,400	over £31,400	over £30,500

Once the starting rate income band has been used, *savings income* (excluding dividends) is taxed at 20 per cent (not basic rate) if you are a basic-rate taxpayer; once your income takes you into the higher-rate band, then savings are taxed at 40 per cent. *Dividend income* is taxed at 10 per cent for basic-rate taxpayers and 32.5 per cent for higher-rate taxpayers.

	2005–2006	2004–2005	2003–2004
Capital gains tax			
Exemption limit	£8,500	£8,200	£7,900
Inheritance tax			
Exemption limit	£275,000	£263,000	£255,000
VAT standard rate	17½ per cent	17½ per cent	17½ per cent
VAT turnover level:			
registration	£60,000	£58,000	£56,000
deregistration	£58,000	£56,000	£54,000
	from 1.4.2005	from 1.4.2004	from 10.4.2003
Personal allowance	£4,895	£4,745	£4,615
Age allowance			
Aged 65–74: personal	£7,090	£6,830	£6,610
Married Couple's	*†£5,905	*†£5,725	*†£5,565
Aged 75 personal	£7,220	£6,950	£6,720
and over: Married Couple's	*†£5,975	*†£5,795	*†£5,635
Minimum amount	*£2,280	*£2,210	*£2,150
Income limit	£19,500	£18,900	£18,300
Blind Person's Allowance	£1,610	£1,560	£1,510

Notes

*Relief restricted to 10 per cent; †available only to couples where either the husband or wife was born before 6 April 1935 or where one person born before that date has married on or after 6 April 2000.

State Pension for women

The State Pension age for women is to be increased to 65; this is being phased in over a ten-year period between 6 May 2010 and 6 March 2020 as shown below.

Any woman born after 6 March 1955 will not be able to draw the State Pension until she is 65.

Pension age for women born after 5 April 1950

Date of birth	Pension age (year/month)	Pension date
6 April 1950 – 5 May 1950	60/1	6 May 2010
6 May 1950 – 5 June 1950	60/2	6 July 2010
6 June 1950 – 5 July 1950	60/3	6 September 2010
6 July 1950 – 5 August 1950	60/4	6 November 2010
6 August 1950 – 5 September 1950	60/5	6 January 2011
6 September 1950 – 5 October 1950	60/6	6 March 2011
6 October 1950 – 5 November 1950	60/7	6 May 2011
6 November 1950 – 5 December 1950	60/8	6 July 2011
6 December 1950 – 5 January 1951	60/9	6 September 2011
6 January 1951 – 5 February 1951	60/10	6 November 2011
6 February 1951 – 5 March 1951	60/11	6 January 2012
6 March 1951 – 5 April 1951	61/0	6 March 2012
6 April 1951 – 5 May 1951	61/1	6 May 2012
6 May 1951 – 5 June 1951	61/2	6 July 2012
6 June 1951 – 5 July 1951	61/3	6 September 2012
6 July 1951 – 5 August 1951	61/4	6 November 2012
6 August 1951 – 5 September 1951	61/5	6 January 2013
6 September 1951 – 5 October 1951	61/6	6 March 2013
6 October 1951 – 5 November 1951	61/7	6 May 2013
6 November 1951 – 5 December 1951	61/8	6 July 2013
6 December 1951 – 5 January 1952	61/9	6 September 2013
6 January 1952 – 5 February 1952	61/10	6 November 2013
6 February 1952 – 5 March 1952	61/11	6 January 2014
6 March 1952 – 5 April 1952	62/0	6 March 2014
6 April 1952 – 5 May 1952	62/1	6 May 2014
6 May 1952 – 5 June 1952	62/2	6 July 2014
6 June 1952 – 5 July 1952	62/3	6 September 2014

Date of birth	Pension age (year/month)	Pension date
6 July 1952 – 5 August 1952	62/4	6 November 2014
6 August 1952 – 5 September 1952	62/5	6 January 2015
6 September 1952 – 5 October 1952	62/6	6 March 2015
6 October 1952 – 5 November 1952	62/7	6 May 2015
6 November 1952 – 5 December 1952	62/8	6 July 2015
6 December 1952 – 5 January 1953	62/9	6 September 2015
6 January 1953 – 5 February 1953	62/10	6 November 2015
6 February 1953 – 5 March 1953	62/11	6 January 2016
6 March 1953 – 5 April 1953	63/0	6 March 2016
6 April 1953 – 5 May 1953	63/1	6 May 2016
6 May 1953 – 5 June 1953	63/2	6 July 2016
6 June 1953 – 5 July 1953	63/3	6 September 2016
6 July 1953 – 5 August 1953	63/4	6 November 2016
6 August 1953 – 5 September 1953	63/5	6 January 2017
6 September 1953 – 5 October 1953	63/6	6 March 2017
6 October 1953 – 5 November 1953	63/7	6 May 2017
6 November 1953 – 5 December 1953	63/8	6 July 2017
6 December 1953 – 5 January 1954	63/9	6 September 2017
6 January 1954 – 5 February 1954	63/10	6 November 2017
6 February 1954 – 5 March 1954	63/11	6 January 2018
6 March 1954 – 5 April 1954	64/0	6 March 2018
6 April 1954 – 5 May 1954	64/1	6 May 2018
6 May 1954 – 5 June 1954	64/2	6 July 2018
6 June 1954 – 5 July 1954	64/3	6 September 2018
6 July 1954 – 5 August 1954	64/4	6 November 2018
6 August 1954 – 5 September 1954	64/5	6 January 2019
6 September 1954 – 5 October 1954	64/6	6 March 2019
6 October 1954 – 5 November 1954	64/7	6 May 2019
6 November 1954 – 5 December 1954	64/8	6 July 2019
6 December 1954 – 5 January 1955	64/9	6 September 2019
6 January 1955 – 5 February 1955	64/10	6 November 2019
6 February 1955 – 5 March 1955	64/11	6 January 2020
6 March 1955 – 5 April 1955	65	6 March 2020
6 April 1955	65	6 May 2020

Note:
The State Pension a woman receives, whether based on her own or her husband's contributions, counts as her income for tax purposes. If a husband receives a dependant's increase for his wife, paid with his pension, this will be taxed as part of his income.

Index